MW01640958

TONY MEISEL

ARCO PUBLISHING, INC.
NEW YORK

Published by Arco Publishing, Inc.
219 Park Avenue South, New York, N.Y. 10003

Library of Congress Cataloging in Publication Data
Meisel, Tony.
A manual of singlehanded sailing.

Includes index.
1. Sailing, Single-handed. I. Title.
GV811.M418 797.1'24 80-22856

ISBN 0-668-04998-7 (Library Edition)

Printed in the United States of America

Acknowledgments

The following have all contributed ideas, encouragement and information: Dick Rath, Tony Gibbs, Gary Jobson, Stafford Campbell, Roger Taylor, Jeff Neuberth, Rod Stephens, Earl Rubell, M.D., Bruce Bingham, Katy Burke and Roger Marshall. I thank them all.

My thanks also to Darlene Pritchard for the time and effort devoted to the illustrations.

Finally, I wish to thank those sailors—on docksides, in waterfront bars, at yacht clubs—who have argued technique and seamanship endlessly, simply for the joys of exercising their orneriness. A finer crew would be hard to find.

Contents

Introduction: Alone at the Helm

Everyone singlehands. Usually you just don't realize you're doing it. When you go out for a daysail or a cruise to a nearby port, you probably raise sail, leave the mooring, make passage, navigate and arrive with little or no help. Sure, you may have crew, and you may depend on them now and then, but the essential operation of the vessel is in your hands.

A Manual of Singlehanded Sailing gives you hard information, based on my own experience and that of many other singlehanders, on how to better manage and operate your boat without the reluctant aid of others. This is not a book for would-be Slocums or Chichesters, though the information still applies. Rather, it is for the average sailor of reasonable accomplishment who wishes to cruise along the coast, with an occasional foray offshore.

It will show you how to use your present skills to make safe, swift passages solo—and how to add to your storehouse of knowledge and techniques, to do alone what you have traditionally thought you needed others to help with. You'll learn how to economically modify your deck layout and rig to make your boat a safe, easily managed platform. You'll learn to plan ahead and think out all your maneuvers—along with alternatives—for every possible contingency. You'll learn to ship out day and night with confidence.

This manual will help sharpen techniques for changing headsails, rigging self-steering, reefing, anchoring, mooring and docking, and maintaining your boat by yourself. You will even come to feel comfortable about docking under sail—with practice. Most important, you will gain confidence in your abilities and in yourself.

Obviously, all of this demands time and practice, and there are no guarantees at sea. But you will slowly begin to understand the lure of solo sailing—the pleasure of a warm evening at the helm, the knowledge and satisfaction that you've made a safe and successful landfall, and no one has done it but you, your hands, your brain, your instincts. In a crowded, inflationary, mechanically inept world, that is satisfaction indeed. To weather a storm at sea and make port is one of the great thrills of a lifetime. You earn the kind of self-esteem that is very rare today.

Furthermore, even with others along for the ride, you will, through your experience, know what to do, no matter what. And there may be times when you are the only one who can bring the ship home safely. *A Manual of Singlehanded Sailing* won't get you to hell and back, but it may help you avoid hell altogether.

Tony Meisel

1
Boat Types and Rigs

If you already have a boat, and intend to keep it, read the next chapter. If you're in the market, and plan to do a lot of sailing alone, keep reading . . .

What I'm about to discuss has been covered by hundreds of experienced sailors, builders and designers before, and probably better, but for what it's worth, I'm going to throw my two cents in. Sloops, cutters, ketches, yawls, catboats, schooners—these are the basic rig types. They can be mounted on assorted hulls, with different keel and rudder configurations, and they all work with a greater or lesser degree of efficiency. What we're concerned with here is rig *efficiency* balanced against *ease of handling*. After all you won't have a brace of hands for each sheet and halyard.

Simplest of all are catboats, but their suitability for passage-making is severely hampered by their inherent lack of balance and poor windward ability. Two-masted rigs of any sort add mechanical complication, expense, windage, and diminished ability to point. That leaves us with sloops and cutters. A cutter is not a sloop with an inner forestay! If you look at the drawings below, you'll see what I mean.

The center of effort of each is radically different due to mast position and the increased sail area in the foretriangle of the cutter. A cutter under main alone will probably have greater lee helm than a sloop under the same sail. However, the textbook dictum about handling under main alone can be thrown out these days. Foresails are so efficient and easily handled that, for safety if nothing else, how a boat behaves under jib or staysail is probably most important. Besides which, mains have shrunk to less that 50 percent of total working area on most boats.

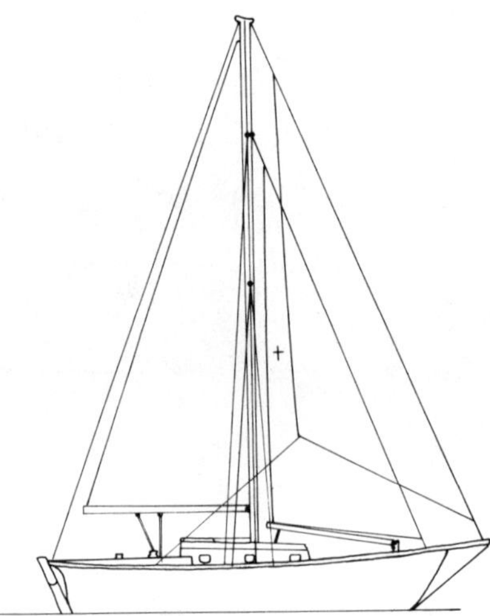

Figure 1. Profile plan of a cutter. This particular type carries a bowsprit and club jib. Note the relative lengths of the foots of the main and the foretriangle. (*Shannon 28*)

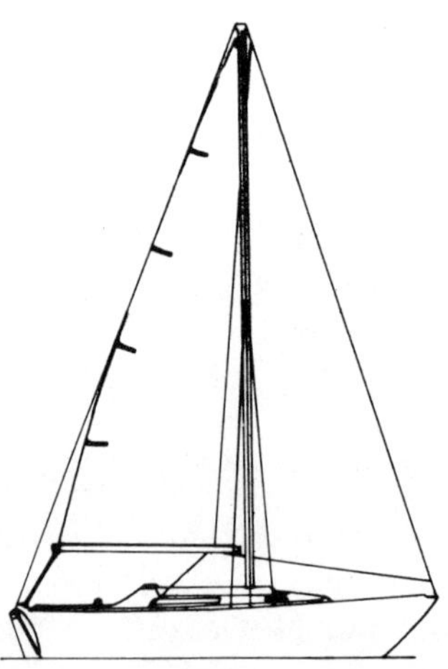

Figure 2. Profile plan of a masthead sloop. Simplicity is the key. Sail combinations are not as varied as those of a cutter, nor is balance as easy to achieve. Still, simple is good. (*Nicholson 31*)

Single sticks have a host of advantages: simplicity, versatility, minimum windage, windward efficiency and less expense, and the thought of losing a mast and being left with nothing can be softened somewhat by jury rig planning. But that's not our concern here.

Most offshore sailors have come to appreciate the advantages of the cutter, its sail combinations and the ability to easily and quickly balance the sails for varying conditions. Even crusty Eric Hiscock has finally come around. Up to about fifty feet LOA, there is probably no competition. Even on small boats, twin headsails can smooth things out. Witness John Letcher's *Aleutka* and Chuck Paine's *Frances* class. Though the sloop is a little less complicated, it is not nearly as versatile.

One of the proponent cries of "cutter folk" is the self-tacking staysail. Having undertaken a few long passages with this rig, I am not totally happy with it. Club booms are potentially dangerous and add to deck clutter. Furthermore, an overlapping staysail, free-footed, is a hell of a lot more efficient. Club sails are useless off the wind, less than overwhelming to windward and okay on a reach. Of course, the lack of boom means another set of winches and more sheets, but the advantages for pure sailing enjoyment outweigh the minor extra work, to my way of thinking. Also, you can set other sails from the inner stay for certain conditions.

The simplest arrangement is to have a removable inner stay, attached to the deck by a Hyfield or similar lever. The stay is braced, not by runners, but by shrouds running aft from the stay attachment point on the mast. This gives permanent strength without the bother of jumper struts or running backstays. The inner stay should be reasonably well separated from the forestay—by at least two to three feet—for easy tacking of the jib or yankee.

You will need two sets of leads, both port and starboard, of course. Try to get the yankee cut lower than usual, to keep the sheet from running so far aft that turning blocks are needed. A slightly larger yankee can be arranged for reefing, cutting out the need for an intermediate genny. I don't like turning blocks; they increase chafe, put enormous strains on the deck, and one once exploded on me. Not a pretty sight!

The staying of a cutter rig, or any rig for that matter, is of paramount importance. Rig strength is determined by spar section, compression strength and resistance to mast bend. That is, ideally

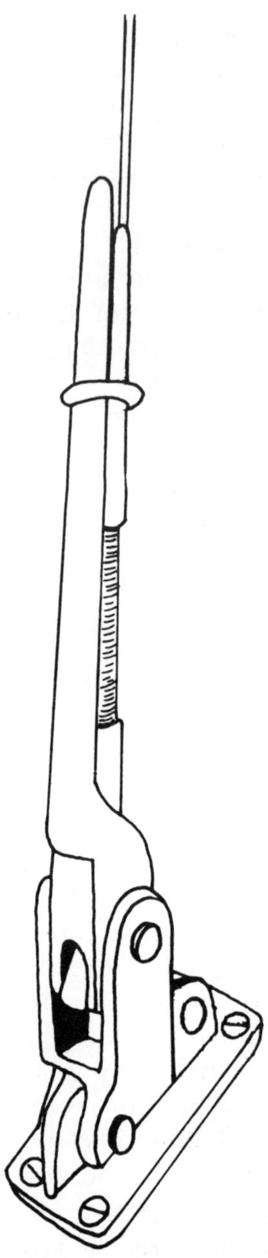

Figure 3. A modified Hyfield lever, without tensioning apparatus. With this arrangement the staysail stay, or inner forestay, may be uncoupled at the deck to allow for ease in tacking genoas and other light air sails.

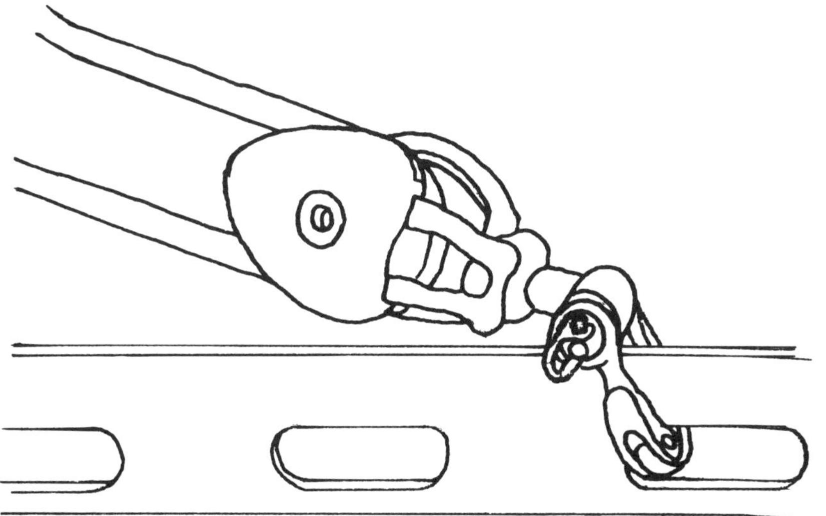

Figure 4. Turning blocks or snatch blocks, used for the same purpose, are subject to double loads and are thus highly susceptible to sudden failure. Caveat emptor!

the stick should stay upright and straight while the rigging and heel of the mast absorb the stresses and loads.

In keeping a mast in a boat, the standing rigging acts as a web support. It allows the fore-and-aft and athwartships alignment of the spar. Unfortunately, it also pushes the mast downward with enormous force. This force must somehow be absorbed. The most effective arrangement has the mast stepped directly on the keel. This does *not* mean butted up against the lead ballast.

The keel in traditional wooden construction served (and still does, of course) as the backbone to which all the structural members of the ship were tied. The ballast in turn was bolted to the keel. In a properly engineered—and few are—modern fiberglass boat there is a system of longitudinal and transverse members (wood, foam, hollow glass sections) glassed into the boat along with bulkheads and deck to form a monocoque structure. These internal stiffeners serve the same functions as did keels, ribs, clamps and shelves of yore. In too many boats today there is little evidence of reinforcing structural members and hence, less than optimal strength for offshore work.

A classic case is Webb Chiles' experience, related in his book *Storm Passage*. His stock 37-foot cutter was without stringers or a floor pan. In his round-the-world voyage, the compression of the mast in heavy weather caused a rupture of the keel and massive leaking, almost causing him to founder.

If you are taking a boat offshore, you can be sure that the forces the mast and rigging will place upon the structure of the boat will be massive. That compressive force must be effectively absorbed without sacrificing smartness under a press of sail, or the watertight integrity of the hull. Provided the keel is structurally part of the boat, it can best absorb those strains. Therefore, a keel-stepped mast, or one thrusting upon a web floor system, is best. Deck-stepped masts are convenient, cheaper and, consequently, more widely used, and allow for a more weathertight deck. However, the deck must be carefully reinforced at the heel of the mast, and there must be a substantial bulkhead directly underneath or a mast compression pillar in the same location. Still, you sacrifice ultimate strength.

Standing rigging deserves equal consideration. The practice of a few years ago—forestay, backstay, uppers, double lowers—is hard to beat. With a cutter, add an inner forestay with either runners, jumpers or additional aft lowers.

Modern racing practice has had its influence, and not all to the good. However, the super-rigs of Tim Stearns or Ridder and Bergstrom don't concern us here. Hydraulics, triple spreaders, bendy masts and such have no place on a cruising boat. We're after simplicity.

Swept-back spreaders, babystays and fractional rigs are less demanding in terms of compression but have certain disadvantages for cruising. They cause chafe, and if one stay goes, the whole rig will probably topple over the side. Remember, you are alone. There's no one else to twang strings and fiddle with backstay adjusters. Nothing, for the committed cruising man, beats masthead rigs for strength and simplicity.

Assuming you accept this solution, certain procedures should be followed to ensure rig integrity. First and foremost, chainplates must be properly anchored and aligned. Once again, the pulling forces put upon them are very great, and they have to be through-bolted to a structural member and glassed in. They must also be of heavy enough section, long enough to distribute the forces, and of reasonable tensile strength to accommodate the bending and twisting—inadvertant or not—that they are subject to. More and more, chainplates are set inboard, which certainly enhances windward performance and, with today's beamy boats, allows spreaders of less than six feet. But it is harder to securely attach them to cabin sides or decks. You often see glass fractures where the plates enter the deck, a sign of probable later trouble.

Having established our anchoring points, and assuming that wire rope will go between the masthead and those points, it might be a good idea to take the time to consider the devices used to attach and adjust the rigging. Long gone are the days of deadeyes and lanyards, wire loops and strap tangs. Now we've got Norseman and Sta-Lock terminals, swaging, turnbuckles, T-ball terminals and rod rigging.

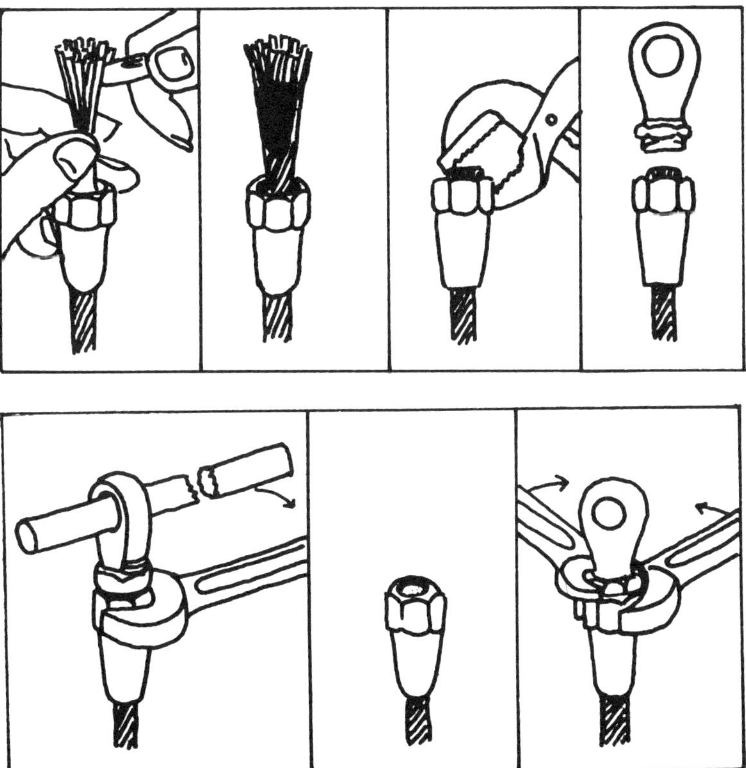

Figure 5. Sta-Lock or Norseman terminals, unlike swaged fittings, can be fitted at sea, following a simple sequence. Manufacturers' instructions must be followed to the letter and it is best to test assemble one with spare rigging wire before attempting the entire rig.

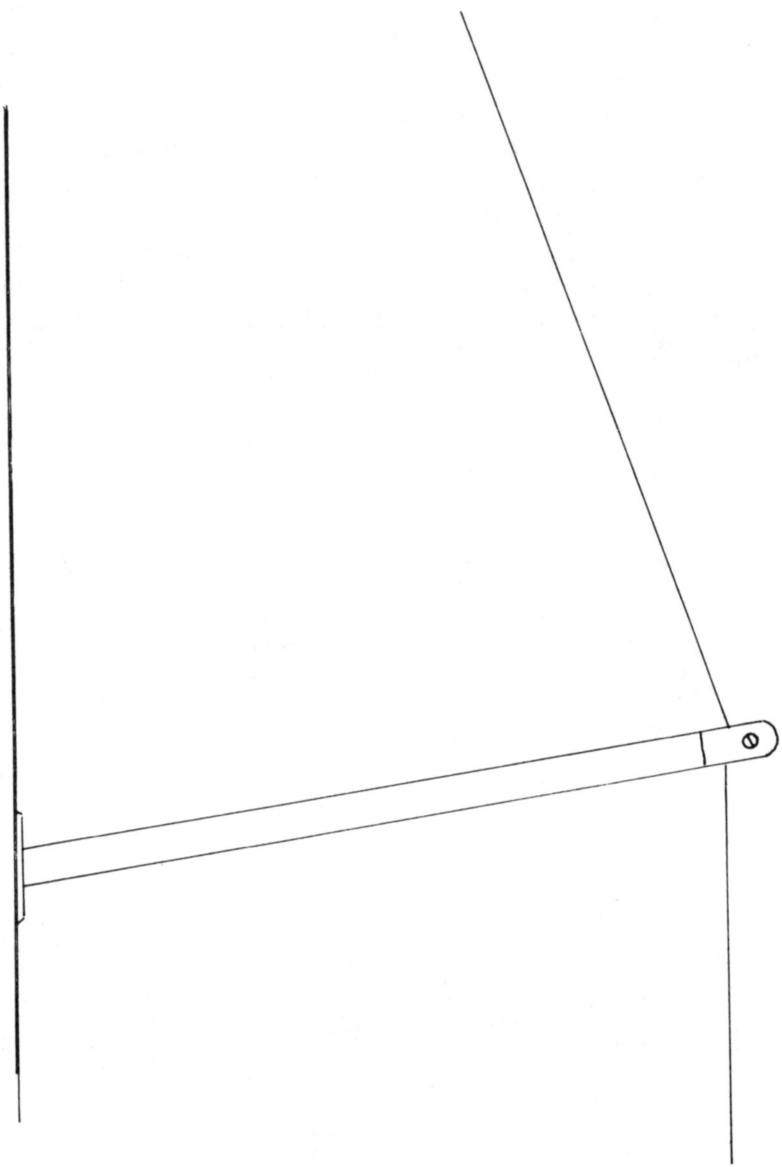

Figure 6. My own boat is fitted with tubular spreaders, the outboard ends of which are fitted with a split, bored and captive slot for the shroud wire. The entire assembly through-bolts to the spreader tube. Such an assembly obviates the need for chafing gear, baggywrinkle or other such aerodynamically inefficient and liable-to-fall-off devices.

Swaging is the norm for attaching end fittings to wire, and it works quite well. For offshore purposes it has one disadvantage. Unless you have a swaging machine or replacement rigging aboard, you can't replace rigging. Sta-Lock and Norseman fittings, and others of the same ilk, such as Castlock epoxy fittings (though I've personally had no experience with these), seem to provide a comparatively simple solution to do-it-yourself rigging, especially in times of rising labor costs. They have been tested to equal the strength of the wire and can be installed with a few simple tools, if you follow instructions carefully.

T-ball terminals are eminently convenient for racing classes and trailer-sailers, but I have seen one rip through a mast wall on one occasion and would prefer not to have them aboard a cruising boat. Rod rigging has no place on a singlehander's boat. It can't be repaired, and you can't very well carry a spare rod. It's expensive and subject to sudden failure, unlike wire, which can be inspected regularly.

Through-bolted tangs smartly pinned with cotters and bolted-on spreaders seem to be the best solution for the cruising sailor. Most spreader ends are terribly designed. There really ought to be a captive device, smooth and rounded, to hold the uppers in position and lessen the need for windage-producing chafe pads.

Currently in fashion are stainless steel turnbuckles. Fine, except for two small items. One, stainless steel is subject—no matter what the grade—to sudden failure from oscillation fatigue, and you can't know beforehand when it will go. Second, stainless turnbuckle threads can gall and bind unless they are the rolled and not the standard cut threads. Hasselfors of Sweden is the only rolled thread rigging screw I know of.

One of the so-called silicon bronzes is probably most reliable for turnbuckle manufacture. Several different bronzes exist and you'd have to be a metallurgist to distinguish between them. The rigging screw market is dominated by an aluminum-silicon-nickel-copper mixture, which works just fine.

I must admit to a prejudice in favor of good, old fashioned fork-and-fork screws because, if your swaged fitting goes, you can more easily rig a jury fitting. The most ingenious design, and one that is suitable, at the moment, only for small boats, is made by Johnson Marine in Connecticut. Based on an L. Francis Herreshoff prototype, it is the essence of sound engineering and simplicity.

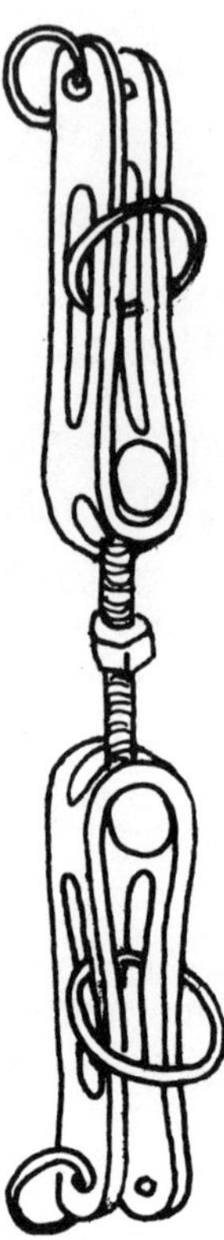

Figure 7. The Johnson turnbuckle. Based upon a rigging screw design of L. Francis Herreshoff, now updated in modern materials, this number does away with the need for toggles, integral or otherwise. An intelligent piece of hardware.

No turnbuckle should be fitted without a toggle. Very few production boats are delivered with toggles, but the rigging does move back and forth thousands of times in a year's cruising, and the stress upon the metal of a turnbuckle is enormous. A toggle, fitted to the lower end, takes care of athwartships as well as fore-and-aft movement.

I can make no recommendations on tuning except to follow your normal practice, but remember that foresails can be cut to allow for some forestay sag. This used to be quite common in Holland, with iron rod rigging on botters, and the English sailmaker Austin Farrar has written about its effectiveness. However, it is rarely done.

2
Decks and Deck Layouts

Every and any boat can be rigged for singlehanded sailing. Obviously, some are easier to handle than others, but neither size nor type of vessel should deter you from giving it a try. There is no perfect way to rig your boat, and anything I suggest is only a starting point.

So let's look at what you've got hanging on the mooring or tied to the dock. Chances are it's a sloop, somewhere between 28 and 35 feet LOA. It's got a forestay, a backstay, uppers and double lowers—inboard rudder, trunk cabin, a few winches, a few cleats, slab reefing, topping lift, working sails and a genny complete the picture.

Standard wisdom has it that all sheets and halyards should be led aft to the cockpit for efficient singlehanding. Not so! This is a super idea if you happen to be lazy, or particularly fond of the cockpit. However, by setting up a configuration of winches, stoppers and blocks, you tend to clutter the deck, set up hazards all over the place and generally complicate matters.

Now, don't take this as gospel. There are occasions when having everything at hand can be a blessing: a full gale offshore or a tight maneuvering situation, for instance. What you have to consider is the extent to which you wish to compromise. For every line led back to the cockpit, at least two blocks will be necessary, not to mention those cleats, stoppers and winches. The major problem is not really obstruction; it's chafe. For example, an internal main halyard can exit the mast through a block, pass through a turning block on deck, wend its way through a couple of fairleads and around a winch, and end up belayed over the edge of the coachroof on a proper cleat (more on this later). Depending on how you count, that's six or seven chafe points. If you leave the whole mess on the mast, you will have to contend with the exit block, a winch and a cleat. And don't for a minute think you don't have to worry about chafe with winches and cleats. They take their toll. The nasty fact is that replacing a halyard at sea can be a lot more difficult than clambering to the mast now and then. But whatever you do, you'll have to weigh efficiency, safety and ease of operation with that most important of seamanlike dictates: keep it simple.

If there are to be any recurring themes in this book, simplicity is the one most likely to be hammered home. Every piece of equipment added on board becomes a contributing factor in the application of Murphy's Law. Furthermore, modern gear is costly and increasingly sophisticated. When it works, it's lovable; when it doesn't, you end up with a boatload of expensive paperweights. And the designers and manufacturers are not really to blame. The sea has spent thousands of years destroying whatever man has placed in its embrace. No matter how hard our alloys, how resistant our synthetics, the sea has it in for us. Without constant care, nothing, absolutely nothing, can survive the ravages of salt, wind and water.

Buy the best and buy the least. It may not make your local dealer happy, but you'll be glad of it in a few months, not to mention years later.

Back to the boat. Increasingly, production boats come with deck-stepped masts. The compression is borne by the bulkhead underneath. For most sailing this works just fine; it solves the problems of mast boot leaks, keeps the mast out of the cabin and, if the mast goes overboard, it can be retrieved (you hope) with little damage. That bulkhead, however, is very vulnerable. Ideally it should be fully glassed to hull and deckhead, the doorway through to the forecabin (the area of greatest stress) should be oval and the frame or surround should be laminated. Even then, potential weaknesses abound.

If possible, find a boat with mast stepped on the keel, and a keel with substantial floors and support. Whichever you have, see to it that there is proper drainage for the foot of the mast and some way to adjust fore-and-aft rake. One further option might be mentioned, one not often seen on American boats but popular in Europe: the tabernacle. Irving Johnson's last *Yankee* was equipped this way, as is Mike Peyton's ketch. Advantages are total freedom from cranes and fixed bridges, and the ability to lower away and undertake repairs yourself. I know of no stock boats so built, but the option exists for modification—if you have the need.

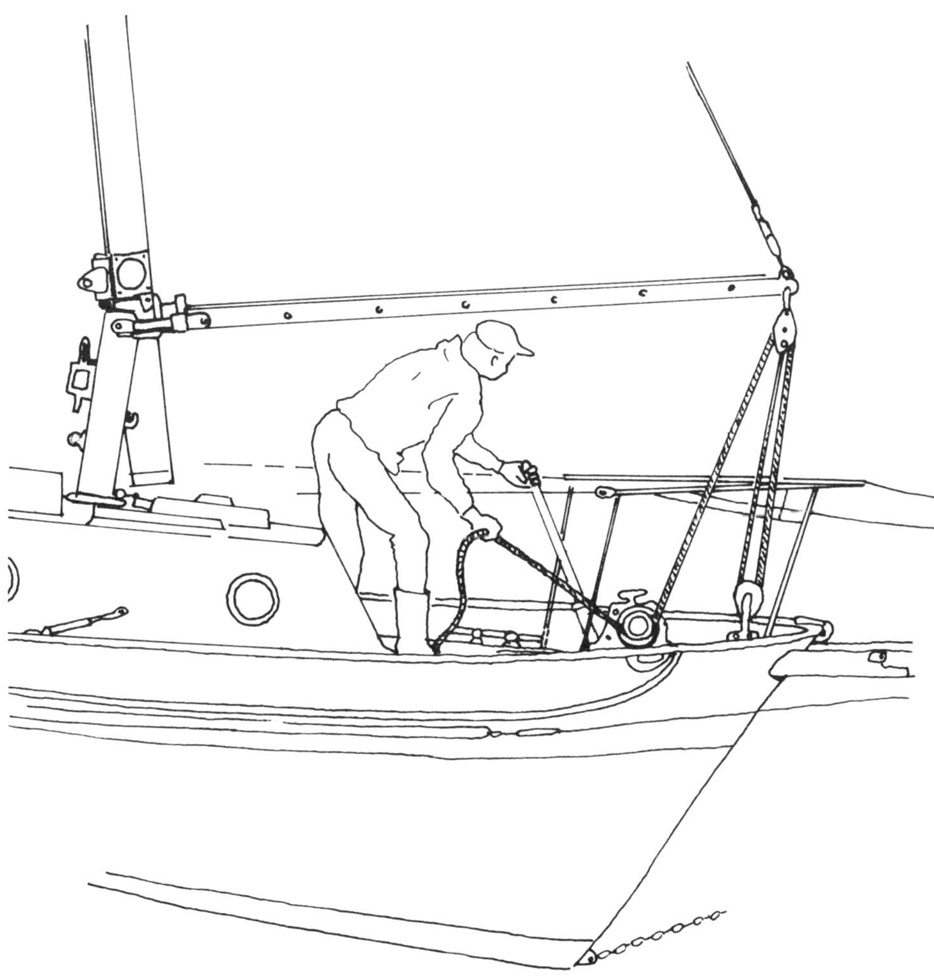

Figure 8. Tabernacles allow for reasonably efficient raising and lowering of masts, a blessing when cruising in areas of low bridges or where cranes are not readily found. A tabernacle also allows for masthead repairs when going up in a bosun's chair would be impracticable.

At a few feet up from the base will be a cluster of winch pads. These ought to be set slightly offset from a beam-on position, made of aluminum or stainless steel, and either welded or attached with self-tapping machine screws, with proper insulating gaskets for both pad and screws. Galvanic corrosion is a real problem, and chances are the mast, not the pad, will be weakened. Also, keep the fittings to a minimum. Too many winches and cleats weaken mast structure. After all, the mast is just a hollow aluminum tube, and if you drill it full of holes in one area you jeopardize the ultimate strength of a vertical strut under enormous strains. Personally, I have no winches on the mast. I use tackles for setting up halyards, along with downhauls for final tensioning. I am in the minority, though, and if you do have halyard winches on the mast, make sure the jib winch is either higher or lower than the main winch and on the opposite side (less chance of localized stress). Cleats should be below the winch, by at least a foot, angled to allow for easing and stopping the line. Fastening procedures are the same as for the winch pads.

Another alternative is clustering the winches on deck at the base of the mast. If you are going to use winches, this may be the best solution. It allows easier handling in heavy weather (your center of gravity is lower), keeps anything from weakening the mast structure and allows you to use the winches for other purposes—for warping alongside from amidships, as an anchor winch and so on.

The last possibility, and the one most beloved by singlehanders, especially the ocean-crossing variety, is leading everything, absolutely everything, back to the cockpit. This involves all the clutter and mechanical complications mentioned above, but it does allow for absolute ease and safety, in that you never have to leave the cockpit . . . perfect for the sedentary, but also immensely energy conserving and safe. If you opt for this, single winches on either side of the companionway, with stoppers just ahead on the coachroof, is the most economical and efficient way of doing things. Don't forget that winches are heavy, so the fewer up high, the less windage and the lower the center of gravity.

You may have noticed we're working our way back to the cockpit. Here's where you spend most of your time, relaxing, drinking, eating, making love, screaming at your wife/mistress/children/crew—and actually sailing. No cockpit is ideal, a reality you will just have to learn to live with. If it's big enough to lounge around in, it's too big for ultimate seaworthiness. If it's too deep, being pooped can be dangerous. If you allowed yourself to buy a vessel without a bridgedeck, you run the risk not only of taking green water below but also of weakening the deck structure. With a tiller, you crowd things, and with a wheel you add to mechanical complexity, as most wheels are placed with an eye to crew operating winches and other contrivances. My own prejudice (not carried out to perfection on my own boat) would be for a set-up similar to that of the *Great Dane*, a 28-foot sloop of docile performance but great thoughtfulness, designed by the late Aege Utzon.

The rudder is transom-hung, the helmsman's seat is raised, four large cockpit drains keep things dry, the winches can be operated by either helmsman or crew, the mainsheet comes to hand while at the helm, and the compass can be read from any part of the rather small cockpit.

The Great Dane cockpit is perfect for a small singlehanded boat for *me*. Maybe not for you. Like a cheesecake and art, no one agrees, or has to, on matters of taste, and boats are irrational mistresses. Jim Crawford, who built *Agantyr* and sailed her singlehanded for thousands of miles, designed the boat with no cockpit at all, though he was perhaps more interested in ultimate seaworthiness than most of us. However, since the aft end of any boat we will use is going to have a well in it, let's go about using it as best we can. For the singlehander, the primary concern is having everything at hand, like a good galley. The less effort expended getting from one activity to another, the better. The key word is activity, for you alone can decide what is most important to you and what is done most often. Thus my notion of keeping halyards at the mast. How often do you hoist sails in relation to trimming sheets or moving the tiller or wheel? Just as you have the radio below (to keep it safe, and dry as well) because it is not used every five minutes, so you need the compass in the optimal viewable spot.

In the Trades, a boat can be allowed to sail itself for a couple of thousand miles. Most of us, cruising for a few weeks in coastal waters, can't experience the luxury of steady winds—and untouched sails. We can't inspect rigging at our leisure and sit in the cockpit working fancy rope patterns for galley mats. Sailing is fun, but it is work too. Don't forget that. You plan your landside work and the procedures to best accomplish it, so you must plan your sailing. You should know beforehand the steps necessary to change a headsail or anchor the boat. And you should practice. You couldn't become

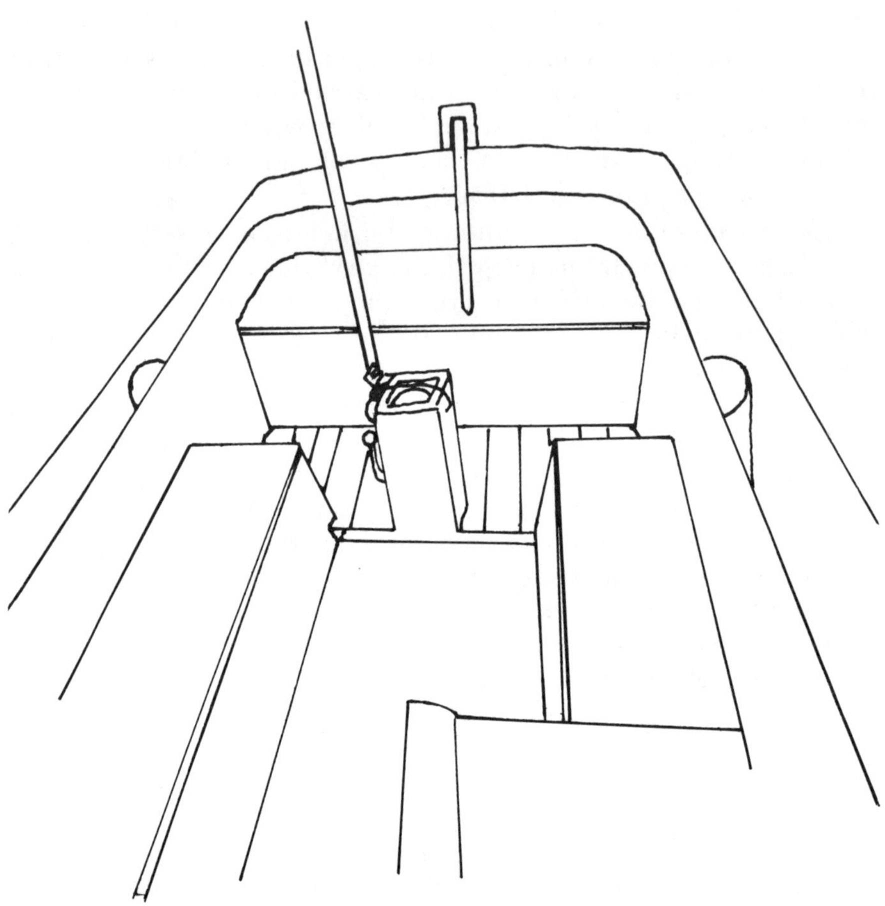

Figure 9. The *Great Dane* cockpit. Like so many intelligent and sensible designs, this one is now defunct. Nevertheless, it is a prime example of good ergonomics. Everything is at hand: the teak pillar acts as both compass binacle and mainsheet termination and has the engine controls mounted on its starboard face; the helmsman sits slightly above the crew, with tiller at hand and winches accessible to both himself and anyone forward (shown by base supports); not shown are the four cockpit drains and the high companionway sill.

a concert pianist without practice, and you cannot become a good sailor without practice, either. I have spent years arguing with my racing friends that seamanship is not getting the most out of a boat to windward, but getting the boat and crew to their destination safely. It is waterborne management. And it is a collection of techniques . . . none of which comes naturally. Practice, practice, practice. We all know the performance is better than the rehearsals, but unless you know your lines by heart, you won't be able to bring it off. We all know the drill about throwing a life preserver overboard, jibing, and retrieving it. On a calm day, try throwing your least favorite kid overboard and try getting him back on board!

What, you ask, does this have to do with singlehanding, and the cockpit? If you are alone in the cockpit, you must be able to do anything required without having to take the time to find things, set up devices or plan maneuvers. Contingency planning must be done, and the logical place to start is with the arrangement and modification of the cockpit.

Let's begin at the bottom and work our way up. Production boats, with the exception of a very few, have inadequate cockpit drains. Assuming you get pooped, how much water would the cockpit hold? 50 gallons? 100 gallons? At 8 pounds per gallon, that's a lot of weight dragging the stern. If your boat has the standard two ¾- to 1½-inch drains, it will not empty fast enough to bring up the stern before another wave fills the well again. This can not only soak you and everything else, it can bloody well sink your ship. I feel that four 1½-inch drains should be installed, one at each corner, flush with the sole and with cross bars over them. Grates obstruct more than they allow through. The drains should drain overboard through double-clamped reinforced hoses and seacocks that can be reached without jeopardizing the watertight integrity of the cockpit.

In boats with cockpits extending to the transoms, direct ports through the stern above the waterline are best, with neoprene flaps fitted to the outside of the transom to keep the water going out rather than in.

Next up, usually to starboard of the helm, are the engine controls. Today these are clever single-lever arrangements. I remember that, in my father's boat, to shift from anything, a bronze deckplate was flipped open, a long, lethal bronze lever inserted and brute force applied, usually resulting in permanent damage to ego, body or boat, or combinations thereof. These controls need little in the way of care except lubrication and tightening now and then. However, the accompanying electrical connections for ignition, switches, starting plugs and such are highly vulnerable to water, spray, mist, bumps and knocks. If they are behind a Plexiglas panel, the panel should be gasketed and capable of being securely fastened. Instruments should be high enough (especially engine instruments) to be both visible and clear of any volume of water that might fill the well.

When you bought your boat, the salesman no doubt told you about the wonderfully capacious cockpit lockers: "They'll hold everything." They probably do. And they should not only be gasketed and sealable against being thrown open in a knockdown, they should also be organized. All those lines, fenders, sails, spares, oars, anchors and objects best described as junk are ostensibly there for a purpose.

Stock boat builders do not generally do anything with locker space. It is too damn expensive. Thus you are left with one, two or three holes, deep holes at that, that have an uncanny way of collecting water in those corners where chain rusts away or awnings mildew and molder. Just imagine being forced to live in a cockpit locker for 24 hours. Enough said?

Lockers should be divided horizontally and vertically. Use a grate for the bottom division to keep large items out of the bilge water. Then make vertical partitions to segregate odds and ends so that what you use most is easily accessible, what you rarely use is easy to get to and what you never use, throw out! Try to keep the aft end of the lockers free of anything but fenders and other such lightweight gear. Heavy items drag down the stern, making for hard steering and sluggish handling. Don't put the outboard in the lazarette or afterlocker. Every added bit of weight hampers sailing characteristics, and way aft is the worst place possible to put anything.

The most important gear in the cockpit, as far as the singlehander is concerned, are the mainsheet and jibsheet arrangements. Both must be at hand to the helmsman, for the lone sailor must be able to control all three with minimum movement and as little fouling as possible.

Cockpit arrangement is the area in which most stock boats fall short of the ideal. Nine out of ten boats on the water are billed as cruiser/racers. They are designed for families and Sunday around-the-buoy charges. They are built with line production and economy

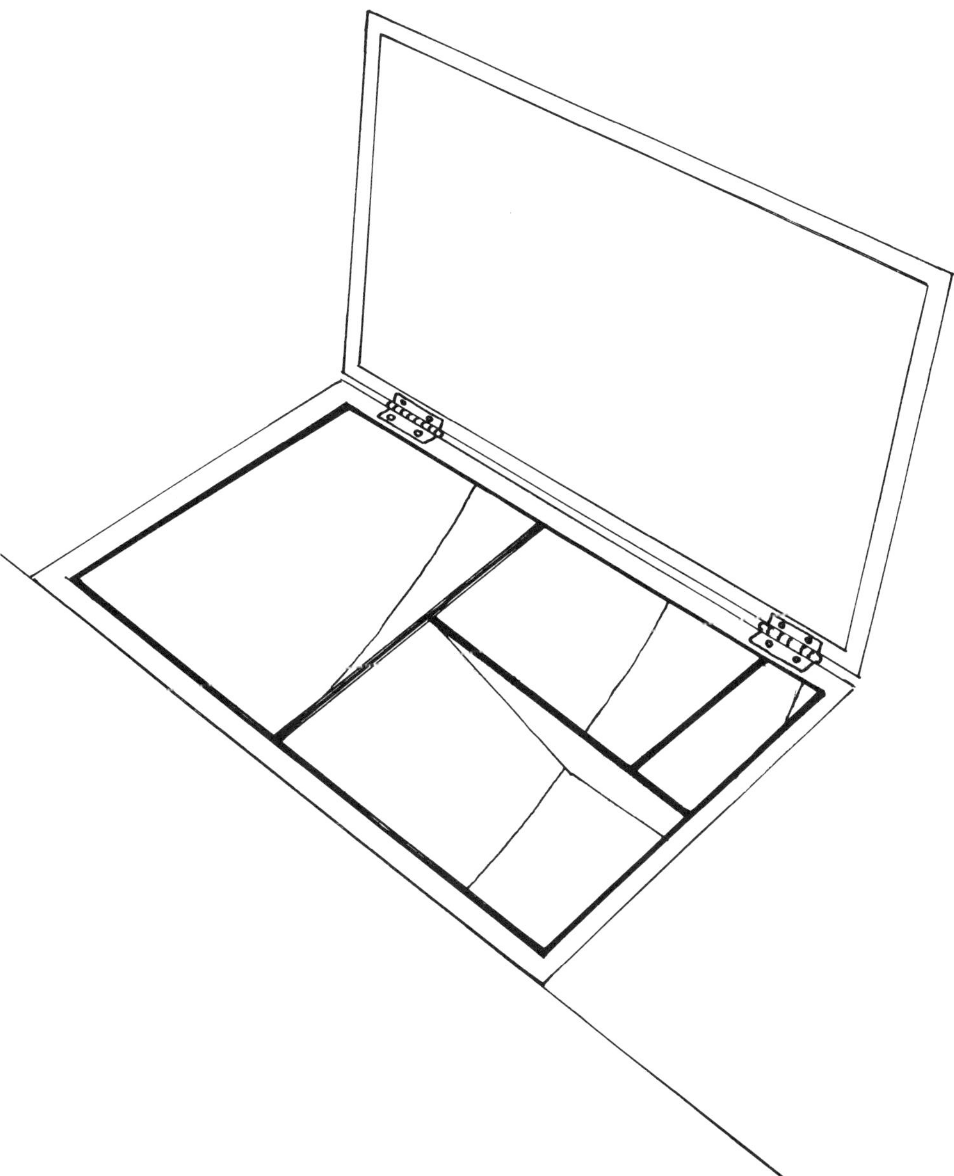

Figure 10. Cockpit locker organization. Horizontal and vertical subdivisions allow organization and ready access. Partitions may be glassed to hull or fitted as removable panels in slotted holders glassed to hull. In either case, allow for limber holes in the bottom edges for decent drainage.

in mind. When the occasion for singlehanding arises, you find you have to run forward to trim the jib, run back to the helm, reach around for the mainsheet, and generally waste time and effort, which you cannot afford alone, accomplishing the most necessary and simple tasks.

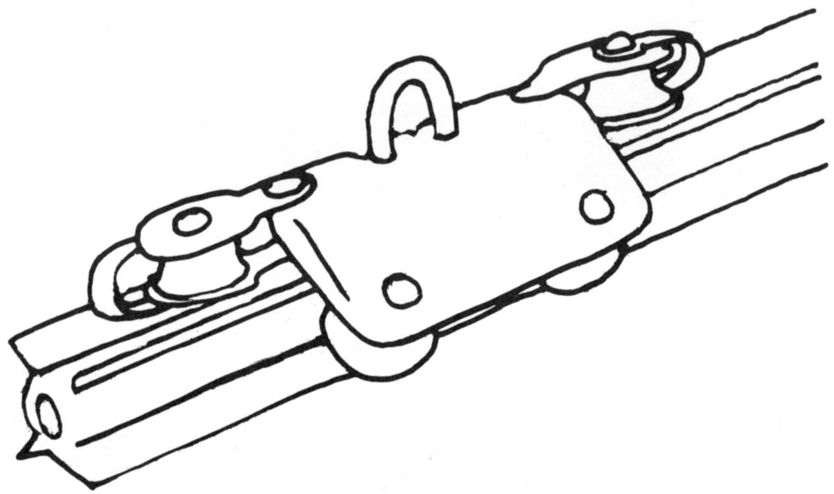

Figure 11. Mainsheet traveler. Many forms exist. The ideal installation should allow for the longest length of track possible, with car adjustment by a simple, multi-part block and tackle arrangement.

The main can be controlled most simply by a multi-part sheet running through blocks at the end of the boom to a cam cleat on the afterdeck. Simple, but does not offer much in the way of control, especially in heavy air. Better yet, run the sheet to a track-mounted, roller bearing car running clear across the aft end of the cockpit. Note "clear across." The longer the track, the easier it is to control mainsail twist. The track should be fitted with extra-heavy end stops, not those little nylon jobbies, and the car should be equipped with control lines leading to cam cleats at either end. Spring-loaded stops are difficult, not to mention dangerous, to adjust in any sort of breeze. Besides, the control lines give added leverage, and any mechanical aid is appreciated when you're alone.

Two other possibilities exist. The first involves running the track across the bridge deck. This is especially useful in a tiller-steered boat. You won't have to reach behind the tiller. Here the sheets are attached to the boom by means of a bail, internal or external. In a long, heavy boom, a tripartite bail system is preferable, in that it spreads the strains. Try to get the lead as vertical as possible, without angles to the deck, when the boom is on the centerline. The second, and even better alternative, is a double-ended sheet, with one end leading to a deck-mounted traveler, the other through a block at either end of the boom. If aft, a cam cleat holds; if forward, the line goes through a block on deck, back to the end of the coachroof and another cam cleat (with a winch in between if you've got yourself a hefty main).

No matter what arrangement you decide upon, make sure that the sheet can be both hauled in and released from the helm position. And use nothing smaller than 3/8-inch Dacron. Anything smaller is impossible to grip under strain with any degree of comfort. Also, use a sheet long enough to permit the boom to swing to a 90-degree angle to the mast.

Often, especially on West Coast boats and on Hinckley's, you'll see a traveler mounted on the coachroof over the companionway hatch. This is a super arrangement except for two little oddments: one, the sheet terminates at the aft end of the coachroof; and two, it may be very difficult to mount a dodger, which is absolutely vital for any hard going to windward.

The options for controlling the jibsheets are legion. If anything, there are too many possibilities—winches, leads, cleats, tracks, cars, blocks, single and double sheets, purchases, and so on. In principle, all you need is something to give you the mechanical advantage to haul in the sail, lead it true for optimum shape and secure it. Sounds simple, yet the modern ocean racer has made the handling of headsails into a game for engineers and mathematicians. It needn't be.

Starting at the clew of the sail, bend on the sheets with bowlines. Sure, shackles are easier. They can also do a splendid job of bashing across your skull when you go forward to change sails. Bowlines are easy to tie, easy to untie. Simple, remember? The options for sheet leads are usually taken care of at the factory: tracks of aluminum or stainless steel, with blocks or cars sliding along their inadequate length. These tracks should be angled, at least six feet long (on a 30-foot boat) and through-bolted. A strong stop at the aft end is a good idea. The slide of the car or block carriage is easiest to use if spring-loaded, but be sure a lanyard is attached. It's damn hard to pull a plunger on a tossing deck with wet hands.

Figure 12. Bowline, the sailor's most useful knot.

Another possibility is individual deck pads with snap-shackle snatch blocks for leads. Such an arrangement keeps the deck clear, although, of course, the positions are extremely important and you cannot allow for infinite adjustments. On small boats, under 25 feet or so, consider using fairleads rather than blocks. They are cheaper, need no maintenance and can be track-mounted. They make no noise either.

One of the omissions on all boats—all—are leads for storm sails. You don't have a storm jib? You may not need it for 10 years, but when you do, there is no alternative. We'll talk about this more in the chapter on sails, but for the moment, let me suggest you hoist the spitfire, work out the leads for it and get them attached—very securely—to the deck. Padeyes will suffice, but the best solution is the screw-in deck block made by the English firm Gibb or those made by Merriman-Holbrook. When the block proper is removed, all you have is a flush-mounted deck plate a couple of inches across. No stubbed toes, no sail snaggers.

Assuming you have the sheet led properly, roughly allowing the sail to be hauled in flat to windward with no apparent distortions, you've got to have some power to actually get it in, and for single-handing, you have to consider the winches you will choose more carefully. First, they must be large, as large as your mounting areas and budget will allow. Of course, you shouldn't get carried away, but one or even two sizes larger than recommended isn't a bad idea. I happen to like aluminum barrel winches rather than bronze. The cost differential isn't so great anymore, and they are much lighter. This is not simply an advantage to top-hamper weight. If you have to repair a pawl or such in a seaway, a bronze drum can hurt a lot more than an aluminum one—and go overboard more easily!

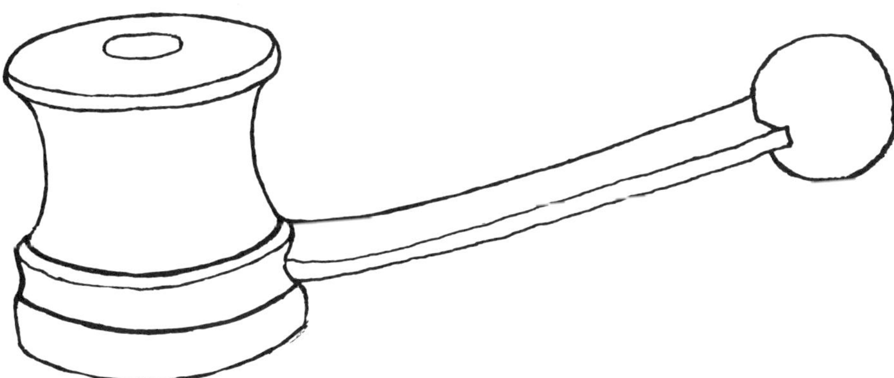

Figure 13. Bottom handle winch. The singlehander's ideal playmate—no handles to lose overboard, no difficulty in throwing off turns.

Winches available on the market: single, two- and three-speed, self-ratcheting, top or bottom handle, self-tailing, self-cleating and so on. I must admit to a weakness for bottom handle winches for singlehanding—no handle to lose overboard, easier to cast off sheets. Also, they are slower in operation and usually less powerful. However, speed isn't of great importance and the loss of power can be compensated for with a larger winch. Unfortunately, the only ones available are by Gibb (in three sizes, for up to 32-footers), Barton and Lewmar (in two sizes). If you have a smaller ship, consider these. Remember, winch handles are expensive, and bottom handle winches are especially handy for use as halyard haulers. No grappling forward with a handle, no stowage problems at the mast.

These are single-speed, very simple winches, with ratchet handles. You can't haul in as fast, but you shouldn't have to, and alone you couldn't anyway.

Next are the workhorses—single- or multi-speed winches with top handles. What I've said about bottom handle winches also applies to these, plus the fact that the higher gear ratios of the second or third speed allow for greater leverage in heavy going. All the major manufacturers put out good products, and they all work just fine. Just remember, you get what you pay for.

Self-tailing and -cleating winches are a commercial development of the past five years. They are marvelously sophisticated mechanical devices. All you do is turn the handle. They grab the rope, keep it moving and hold it. What more could you want? For a singlehander they seem to be the ideal solution. I have my doubts. These jobbies are complicated. That means maintenance and added bother. Also, they grab the rope, causing chafe. No matter what anyone says, additional friction points mean added wear. Finally, they are self-cleating. Since the winch becomes the final resting place for the sheet, enormous strains are put on the fastenings and coaming. I have seen a well-fastened winch rip off its fiberglass base in a gale. Carrying the strain back to a cleat is, in my book, imperative. If you like them, by all means get a pair, but be careful about installation and have back-up cleats, abaft the winches.

Try to install the winch so the sheet leads to the winch from below, at an angle of a few degrees. Otherwise, you'll end up with riding turns and fouled lines. Watch out for potential snags along the lead, and make sure the lead to the cleats is as straight as possible. It used to be fashionable to mount cleats outboard of the coamings—difficult to reach and chafe producing. It is better that we have wide, molded coamings these days.

The number of abominations passed off as cleats today is astounding. Unequivocally, the best cleats are those of the old Herreshoff design—hollow-molded, with a four bolt base. They hold better and chafe less than anything else on the market. Clam cleats slip under extreme strain, cam cleats break and jam cleats can't accept turns.

Now, other patterns exist: the so-called sailboat cleats, horn cleats, wood cleats, wood and metal cleats. They all work, but they all add to chafe to some degree or another. Plastic cleats break, but Tufnol is okay if you can find a good shape. Basically what you want

Figure 14. The Herreshoff cleat. Captain Nat was a master of the obvious; no better cleat has ever been invented.

is something with smooth edges, the capacity to take at least two complete turns and a base that is broad enough to take the strains imposed upon the entire structure.

3
Down Below

At last we can get to the comfort and safety of the cabin, where you sleep, eat, navigate and perform those various private functions so necessary to the maintenance of the human body and spirit. In the past several years, especially since the explosion of sailing upon the popular imagination, "down below" has become synonymous with selling yards of teak, shaggy carpets, cathedral-like headroom, head compartments for orgies and galleys for "gourmet" meals. No one tells the newcomer to the sport that none of the above really is important to the pleasures of sailing and, in fact, a great deal of it is positively detrimental to the enjoyment of a cruise.

Let's start with the requirements of the singlehander: a secure berth, an easy-to-work galley and a dry, stable platform for navigation. And, of course, something with a hole in the top to act as

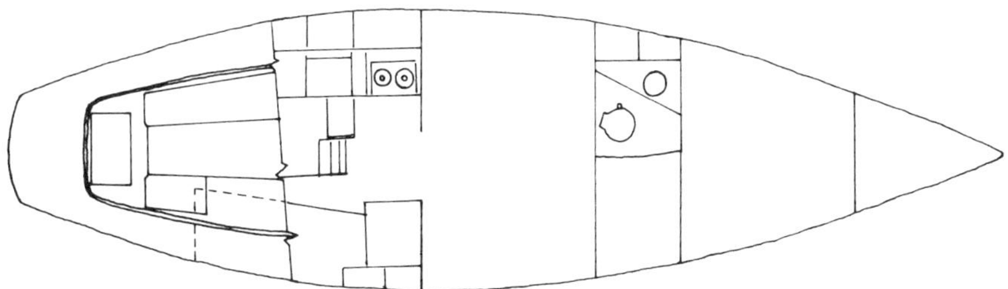

Figure 15. The basic necessities of a singlehander's accommodations. The blank spaces may be filled in with whatever one fancies . . . an aviary, perhaps?

a toilet. In a moderate-sized vessel of standard layout this means a galley to port and a quarter berth and chart table to starboard. The rest of the ship is luxury. All the essential elements for existence are at hand to the companionway, and you can then use the forepeak for sails (it is of dubious quality for much else anyway).

The above takes care of your needs whether on a coastal hop or a transocean passage. The saloon becomes an in-port living room, the head compartment can be used for whatever and you live happily. I say this about the head because it usually is too far from the cockpit for singlehanding. If you have to get on deck in a hurry, you have to fight through the cabin. Much easier to use—and legal these days 3 miles off shore—is the old cedar bucket. (Actually, any bucket will do, as long as you remember to slosh in a third of seawater.) Also, it has the advantage of being useful anywhere.

Figure 16. The cedar bucket. An ingenious device for personal hygiene. Always fill one-third with seawater before use, and empty to leeward, with circumspection.

The chart table can be made more practicable, if of the usual athwartships variety, with a removable fiddle at its outboard edge, a red light above and good holders for pencils, protractors, dividers and such. If much of the quarter berth extends past the companionway ladder, a leecloth becomes necessary, and a plastic sheeting rain shield can be a godsend. Oilskin stowage and boot stowage might profitably be fitted behind the ladder or to one side.

A good idea is to fit racks or shelves either side of the hatch *inside* for binoculars, flares, fire extinguisher and first aid kit.

Galleys are galleys, and most are truly lousy at sea. To eat well you need two burners, a sink with water supply and maybe, just maybe, an icebox. No doubt you'll have a lot more. Some things are nice: fitted racks, a thermos holder, pressure water (spring-loaded faucets, please) and a lined gash bin.

The stove should be gimballed, with room to swing 35 to 40 degrees. It must have rails and adjustable pot holders, and the stove recess should be lined with asbestos-insulated stainless steel. Try to keep all edges of everything well rounded. I remember a cruise on which I was pitched against the galley counter in only a moderate sea and managed to crack two ribs. A safety belt helps, as do proper handholds—vertical, horizontal, everywhere imaginable. You should be able to travel the length and breadth of the cabin with a strong handhold—one that can be gripped through or totally around. Recesses and scalloped drawer pulls don't count!

Also in the galley department: if your sink is the standard 6 inches deep, tear it out and find one at least 9, preferably 12, inches deep. They are not easy to come by, but they make the most secure holders imaginable for bottles, jars, pans and dishes. Make sure it will drain before you invest time and money. I have spent many happy hours in one boat that gurgled and half-filled the sink on starboard tack. Another worthwhile idea is to get rid of the plumbing completely, fill in the through-hull, and cut out the counter to take a plastic wash basin, or, better yet, a standard bucket. When you're through, lift out and heave overboard. With a little ingenuity you will be able to rid yourself of numbers of "modern conveniences," all designed to put holes in the bottom of the boat and to clog with alarming frequency.

The cabin sole is your terra firma for the passage. Make it worthy of your feet. Carpets have absolutely no place on a seagoing boat. They slip, soak up water, and get in the way when you have to dive into the bilges. Unvarnished teak makes the best sole, though it is heavy and expensive. Teak-faced plywood is a good alternative. Whatever you use, do not varnish it! It looks pretty varnished but makes about the most dangerous flooring man could create. Better a non-skid paint. Be sure to bevel the edges of the removable floorboards about 15 degrees, otherwise, when they swell you'll never get them up. Lifting rings should be installed, set flush. You should not need a chisel to lift a hatch. If you can arrange gratings at the foot of the companionway and in the head compartment, all the better.

Underway, even more than at anchor, ventilation is of prime importance. After all, it's nice to be able to breathe. Most American boats are fitted with forward-opening hatches, despite the well-known fact that air is sucked in in reverse. Aft-opening hatches permit circulation beating to windward... in the rain. When it's really pouring, and battening down is imperative, Dorade boxes are the simplest answer, as well as Vetus-type ventilators and sunshine boxes. The last are a Gary Mull innovation, and they seem to work quite well. At sea, centerline hatches are best. Anything off center is asking for trouble in the event of a knockdown.

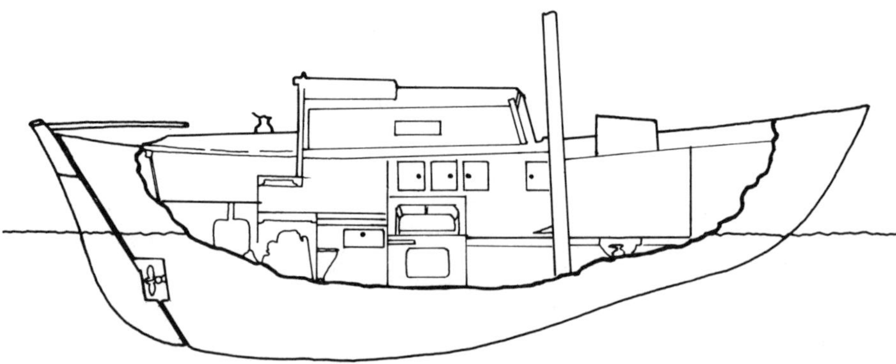

Figure 17. Interior of the *Frances 26*. Headroom is where needed, above chart table and galley, and allows for movement below without getting out of hand aesthetically. Foredeck is left blessedly clear for sailhandling and sunstroke.

Headroom is another cry at the boat show or showroom. Phil Rhodes once said, "You don't have standing headroom in a Cadillac." The only time I've ever really missed it is when at anchor in heavy rain. Otherwise, unless you're an inveterate pacer, standing headroom is a luxury, though it's nice in the galley and heads. Chuck Paine's little 26-footer *Frances* has six feet in the doghouse, and sitting room everywhere else, yet it is one of the most delightful small cruising boats around. You come below, take off your oilies, put on the kettle and check the charts, having to stoop only to go forward to the head or the forepeak berth. Anything over 30 feet and you'll have the headroom unless you measure 6′6″. If that's the case, either be very rich and get a big boat or else lie down.

Assuming you're pretty much stuck with a stock design, how you customize it depends on personal preferences and manias. The important questions to ask yourself are: Does it add to safety? Does it add to efficiency? Does it add to comfort? Most additions add to comfort. Now, I'm all for comfort, but there are limits. And comfort is relative. In heavy weather, warm dry socks are a luxury. In the Caribbean, a freshwater shower can be worth four hundred pairs of socks.

My friend Bruce Bingham, who is certainly one of the most experienced sailors and designers around, believes that only solid leeboards are viable. I, on the other hand, prefer cloth. Why? In the days when sea berths were just wide enough to wedge yourself in and have room for the natural expansion of the lungs, a solid board worked great. But builders realized that most people sleep only at anchor. They made the bunks two feet or more wide. On a hot night, under the enchantment of tropic skies, you need plenty of room to toss and turn in. At sea the opposite is true. With a wide bunk, in any sort of seaway, you'll be tossed from side to side. With a solid board, you court a chance of bruised chest, mangled limbs or a squashed nose. Cloth is resilient—as, hopefully, are you—and will offer greater ultimate protection, provided it is properly sewn and installed.

A "proper" leeboard is made of canvas or Acrilan, of at least 10-ounce weight, with edges doubled and sewn and grommets sewn in (*not* tacked through) on all corners and along both bottom and top edges. The top lines are tied to through-bolted fittings in the cabin top or to the handrails if these exist. The stresses caused by an average body hurtling even eight inches can be astonishing.

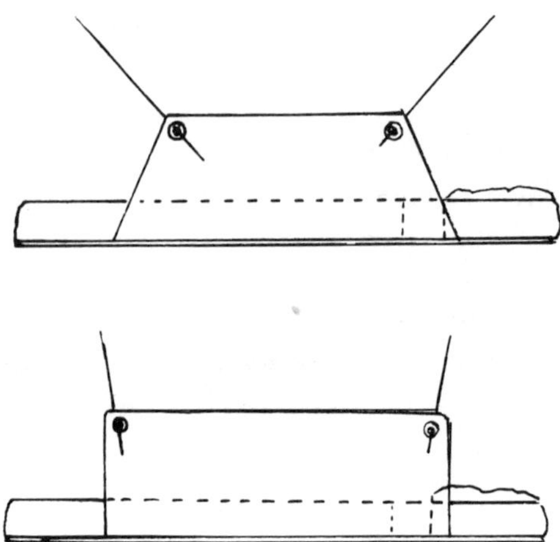

Figure 18. Leecloths. The type pictured at top is far to be preferred. It takes strains better and allows for greater berth ventilation.

When not in use, the whole kit stows under the bunk cushion. Unlike wood, it doesn't warp, rattle, splinter or add weight. It is also much cheaper.

If any locker door is equipped with friction or magnetic catches, carefully unscrew them, carry them topside and drop them overboard to sink into a well-deserved grave. When a locker door springs open, the contents have a tendency to be jettisoned with cruel force. A winch handle hitting you in the head is not amusing. Sometimes it is fatal. The simplest and most secure catches I know of are the old fashioned button catch, either wood or bronze. The type that involves inserting your finger into a hole and pulling it looks neat, but if the boat lurches your finger stands a good chance of coming out mangled and broken.

Locker doors are best installed with the hinges along the bottom edge, for less strain on the hinges and catch. Another good alternative is sliding doors. Popular on Scandinavian boats, they solve the catch problem by doing away with it in toto. And though messier-looking, open-faced bins with netting or shock cord preventers are simplest of all and allow fastest access.

Now the problem of actually functioning below while heeled. A lot of designers and builders seem to think that stuffing the requisite number of berths, galley, head and a few shelves into the shell of a boat creates a seagoing environment. Not so! If you were to take a small table, place a mug of water on it and start to tilt it, at a tilt of about 20 degrees the mug would start to slide. If you also kicked the table, the mug would be flung off and would soak the carpet. If that were a cup of coffee and you were bracing yourself against the table's edge, you would have been scalded. Des Sleighthome, the editor of the British magazine *Yachting Monthly*, recently wrote a very perceptive article about "angles of heel" and brought up some obvious (and rarely noted) points:

First, every flat surface must have stout and high fiddles to prevent athwartship movement beyond the confines of that surface. An inch or two will work in calm conditions, but when the going gets rough, three- or four-inch-high rails are much more practical and useful. As long as they work, they'll do. Nice teak is standard, but a Nicholson yacht I saw recently has aluminum fiddles in the galley, with rounded corners and lapped top edges. Very handsome and very practical too.

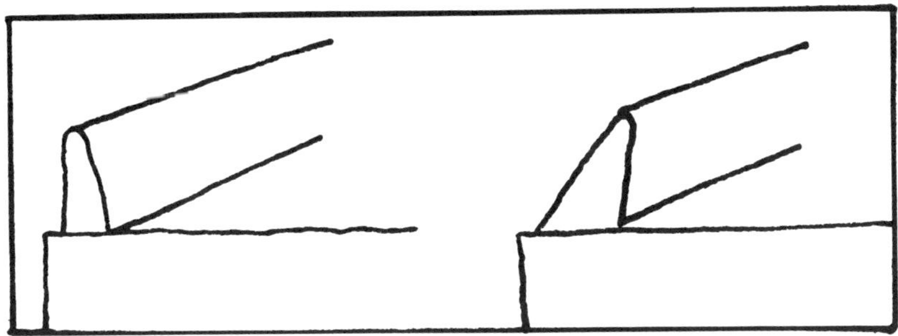

Figure 19. Fiddles. Hand rail on left will allow objects to be jettisoned at extreme angles of heel. Hand rail at right, by presenting a flat surface, won't.

Remember, you're alone and can't hand anyone anything, so be prepared to place things where they will remain until you need them again. Fiddled surfaces or bins are the answer. You very rarely see bins on boats these days, yet they are perhaps the most efficient means of storing things in odd corners. They should have removable covers and some way to fasten the cover securely. In a knockdown, not only will the cover fly, but any contents (like the sextant) will follow, usually with scarifying results.

Second, handholds ought to be as obvious as bannisters on stairs. I was recently cruising on a very expensive production yacht, of impeccable basic construction. Below was not a single rail, pillar, or post, and it was a beamy yacht with a very wide sole. The current trend toward open spaces is fine for latent claustrophobics, but ghastly at sea. You can walk across the kitchen for an onion, but being thrown across the galley into a distant chart table hurts!

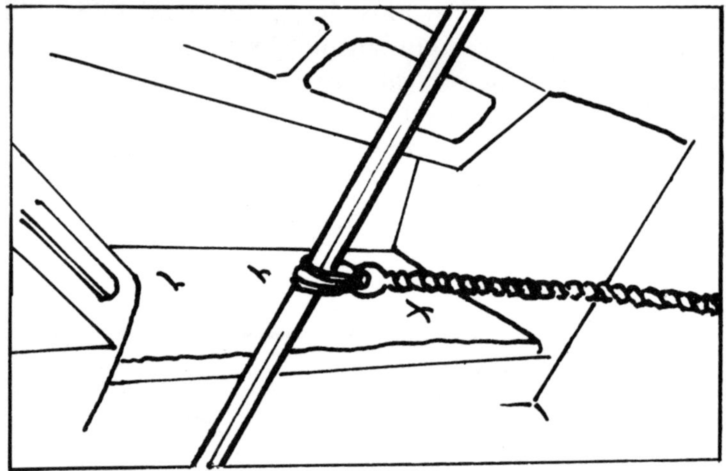

Figure 20. Des Sleighthome's saloon jackline.

If you can, install handholds so you can walk the entire length of the interior without releasing one before you get to the next. Another of Sleighthome's suggestions is a length of nonstretch Dacron strung from a bulkhead pillar to a cockpit cleat. I've tried it this season and it works. Easy to grab, cheap and quickly rigged and removable. Another example of the obvious that you tend never to think of.

4
Sails and Sail Trim

Obviously, your sail wardrobe will depend on the conditions in your regular cruising grounds. A heavy weather main makes as much sense in Southern California as a reacher does in the North Sea. Anything larger than 150 percent genoa is absurd for comfortable singlehanding, though a light reacher or "cruising spinnaker" would be easy to handle for light going. By and large, whatever working sails you have, you'll keep.

Storm sails are another matter. They are a necessity for any serious, that is to say prudent, sailor. And having them is not enough; you must know how to hoist and use them. Here we go with practice again. Both storm jibs and trysails should be triple-stitched, roped all around and of a cloth weight equal to that of the main. Often, old cruising salts will tell you of the need for storm canvas of 12- or 14-ounce cloth. That may have been true of flax sails, but with Dacron the only thing likely to give will be the stitching. Corners must be reinforced.

The storm jib should be fitted with both foot and head pendants of wire, and really positive hanks. In gale force winds, hanks, shackles, knots—you name it—can easily be flogged open. I haven't tried them, but Brummel hooks might be the answer—no moving parts and nothing to hang up on stays or sheets.

If your sailmaker is the gung-ho racing type, and most are, you'll be assaulted with cloths, weights, stretch, warps and wefts, grooved stays and all the paraphernalia of the IOR crowd. Forget it. What you want, and need, are simple, honest sails, well cut, and with the minimum adjustments. Lots of reef points are nice, but forget about stretchy luffs, foot zippers, windows and such. Cloths should be of average weight, soft-finished. Try to stay away from exotica. You are going to have to repair the bits and pieces by

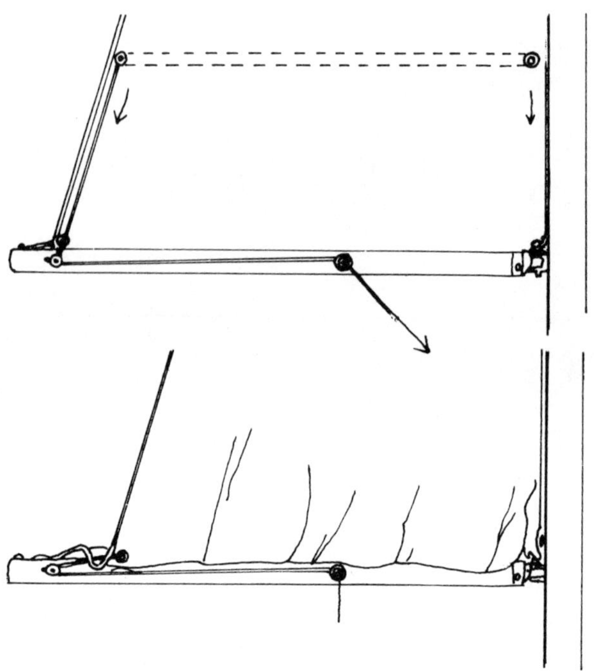

Figure 21. Slab reefing. Simple, easily installed and capable of one-man operation at the mast. Sets far better than any roller arrangement.

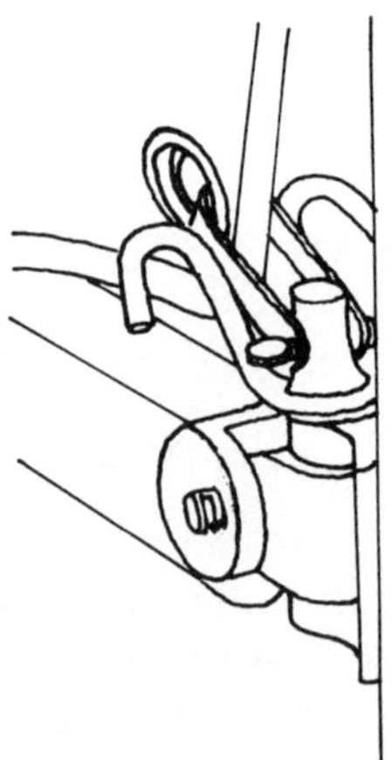

Figure 22. Permanently attached double gooseneck hooks make for quicker reefing.

yourself. Have the headsails fitted with strong piston hanks (not brass) and have them taped to the sail—it makes repairs easier. Grooved headstays are for the fully crewed yachts, not, emphatically not, for the singlehander.

I have always felt, along with Ted Brewer, Bernard Heyman and a few others, that the best cruising rig is overcanvassed. You don't change down, you reef with the advent of a breeze. Mains, as mentioned before, must have at least two sets of reef points. Slab reefing is much to be preferred for the loner. The sail sets better and reefing can easily be undertaken by one soul bound to the foot of the mast. Roller reefing always sags and needs at least two to set up. If you happen to have the halyards leading to the cockpit, it is possible to arrange for reefing lines to be led aft also. Starling Burgess did it for Paul Hammond in the 30s with *Barnswallow* and Ian Hannay used a variant on the *Galion* in the late 60s. Once again, you have the choice of simplicity or ease of operation. Compromise and trade-offs are the keys. It's all a matter of personal preference.

If you're starting fresh, try to persuade your sailmaker to cut all the headsails with compensations for the same lead. He'll have to come aboard and measure a bit, but it means you will be able to install shorter tracks, and will end up with less deck clutter. And the decrease in efficiency is not very great.

Roller furling and roller reefing headsails are a mixed blessing. Furling headsails sag to windward and are exposed, especially at anchor or moorings, not so much to sun deterioration, but to the fury of the wind. Reefing headsails are usually more or less permanently bent on the headstay and, because they must be cut flat, are not the best for off-wind sails. If the sail or gear jams, you're stuck. And you can't well set lightweight running sails or storm canvas unless twin headstays are fitted. However, they're here to stay and are reasonably reliable.

Most sails are influenced in cut by the rating rules, whether IOR or local, and your sailmaker optimizes area because the rules allow it. In a recent conversation with Jeff Neuberth, *Yachting* magazine's resident rigging expert and a very experienced offshore sailor, we got to talking about sails and performance. His opinion is that a few square feet don't really make all that much difference. However, the cut and set make all the difference in the world. For example, a flat-cut, full-hoist lapper will probably take you to windward far more effectively than a full cut, 140 percent genoa. The

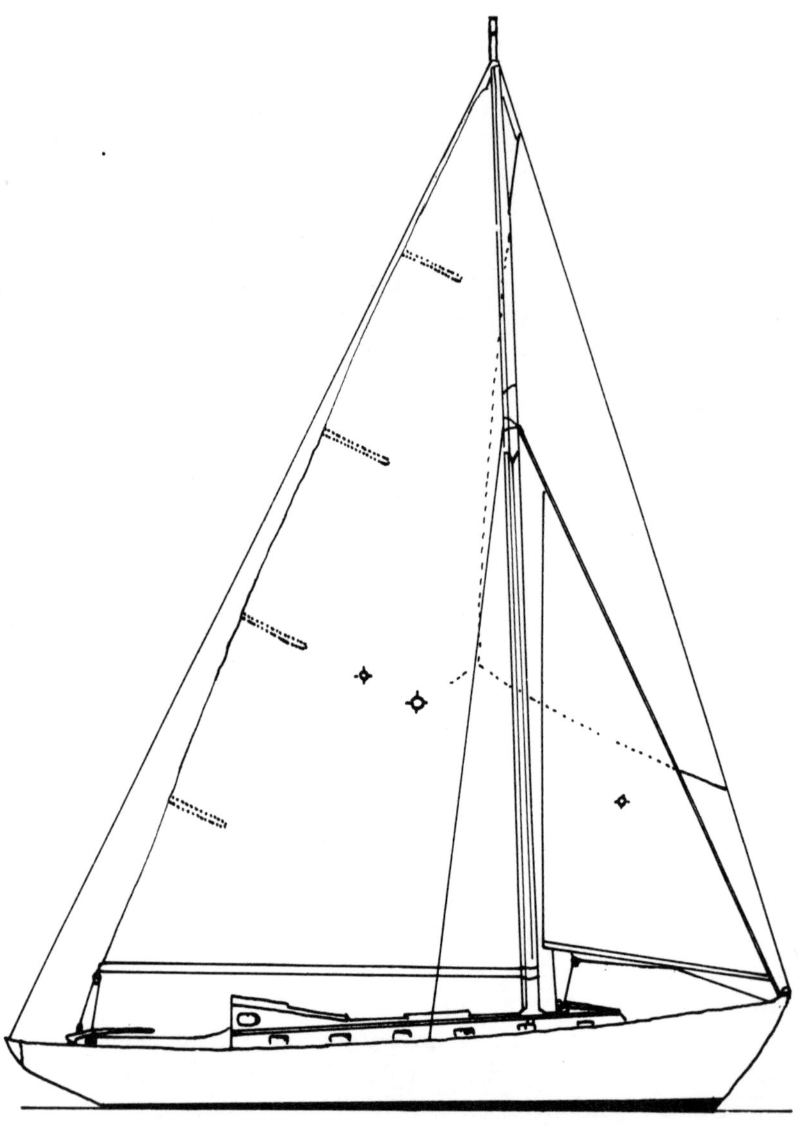

Figure 23. *Barnswallow.* Starling Burgess designed this shoal draft cruising sloop for noted yachtsman Paul Hammond in 1932. Literally every sail-handling line was led aft to the cockpit, all lines were of wire and all were attached to reel winches. Even the staysail was roller reefing. Far ahead of its time, *Barnswallow* may be the first yacht purpose-designed for singlehanding.

similarity to a wing is of greater import in windward sails than is sheer area.

The leading edge presented to the wind is the key factor in windward performance. The higher the hoist, all other things being equal, the higher the boat will point and the greater the speed that will be attained.

On a reach, the above pretty much goes by the board. The sailmaker has to optimize both needs—area *and* efficiency, on several points of sail—to produce a usable sail, unless you wish to cart around twenty sails in the forepeak. Thus, each sail you choose should have the widest range of utility possible correspondent with the greatest efficiency on each possible point of sail. Not an easy task.

Hoisting, lowering and trimming sail aboard a singlehanded boat can be enjoyable or downright treacherous. If you take the time to rig things right, then plan ahead and maneuver yourself and your sails with care, there's nothing to worry about. Too often, a lone sailor will panic, usually in a situation that calls for careful, deliberate action. A good example is coming into an anchorage. You rush forward, drop the jib, stuff it to one side of the foredeck, foul the anchor rode and the entire mess goes overboard, fouling the prop. You are no longer maneuverable, your engine is useless and you could well come to grief. The solution is to drop a second anchor, get the main down and unravel the mess.

However, if you had had the forethought to properly stow the jib in the first place, none of the above would have happened. Sure, push it to one side, but then tie it to the toerail or bag it and secure the bag to the pulpit. The deck is now clear for action and you can sail into that special cove, drop the anchor, back the main to set it and have a cool drink at sunset.

Too often, sail handling ends up meaning lugging lumpy bags around instead of referring to all aspects of moving the sails up, down and *on* the masts. Which brings us to the equipment and techniques of short-handed sail usage. Other than the main, which we will assume is usually left hanked on the ready to raise, of most concern to you is the appropriate sail for the foretriangle. Much of the joy and comfort of your passage depends on this. In the current fashion, headsails are large compared to the main, sometimes in a 2 to 1 ratio. These are for boats meant to rate well and go to windward well. Fine if you have a crew, not so fine if alone. If the design of your boat follows IOR guidelines, take stock. Your main will have a luff-to-foot ratio of 3 or 3½ to 1, and will be very efficient on the wind, fair on a reach and worth a half-knot downwind. On the average, for cruising in temperate areas, you will have to rely on headsails—jibs and spinnakers, or their variants. On Long Island Sound, where I spend much of my time, the winds are light and invariably from the wrong direction.

By and large, no cruising headsail should be a deck sweeper, and I prefer a pendant on all headsails. You won't lose much power, and if you should take green water aboard, the chances of losing that expensive jib will be lessened. Attach it to the deck or stemhead fitting with a snap shackle. I have had far too many screw shackles come undone and become a source of danger in heavy weather. A snap shackle also saves a lot of valuable time when you most need it.

You will find that any genoa more than about 140 percent of the foretriangle area will be a bitch to handle in anything over 15 to 20 knots. The bigger the boat the more this applies. No matter how powerful the winches and how well set the sail, there comes a time when you will have to douse it. Unless you are a Tabarly, your chances of lowering and bagging 400 or 500 square feet of wet canvas without mangling yourself are limited. And bagging even 80 pounds and getting it below can exhaust you.

The solution is to choose, especially in breezes over 12 knots or so, a sail that is one size smaller than one you would use were there crew aboard. A working jib, well cut, can be used over an enormous range. Maybe you'll lose a knot, but you won't be changing jibs every 20 minutes either. Remember, you must conserve energy and strength. Though ideally you ought to attach the sheets to the jib with bowlines, for singlehanding, a snap shackle, such as the Barient one especially designed for the job, makes life easier. Do not use a plunger type with a ring or lanyard that might hang up on the rigging and come undone.

Remember, if you do use a shackle, you're inviting a hit in the head by a flailing clew. A secure fastener with maximum safety is the goal.

Run the sheets back to the cockpit, through whatever fairleads or blocks (properly positioned for that particular sail) you choose, and tie figure-eight knots just short of the ends. You cannot afford a runaway sheet. The sail should still be in the bag, secured to the

Figure 24. Snatch blocks (with universal swivel, or trunnion) are the simplest, most economical means of arranging for multiple sheet leads.

rail or deck. With tack and clew rigged, assess the situation. If you plan to go out under main alone, leave it.

Time to raise the main. Cover off, stoppers off, topping lift secured, mainsheet loosened. Using a locking shackle, haul away. As I have mentioned before, a reel winch has no place on any cruising boat. If you have a wire halyard with a rope tail, make sure the wire takes three or four turns around the winch drum and cleat it. Adjust the downhaul. Go forward again and undo the mooring or prepare the anchor for hauling. If it's blowing, you can short tack up to the drop using the main alone. Sail off!

Sometimes, especially on a mooring, you may wish to get the jib up also, to give you added maneuverability. Raise the main first; then, and only then, raise the jib. It will flog. Release the mooring, move back to the cockpit and winch in the jib. Leave the main alone until you've gathered way. The headsail will supply the drive needed, and the sooner you have it drawing, the sooner you'll stop it flogging the rigging.

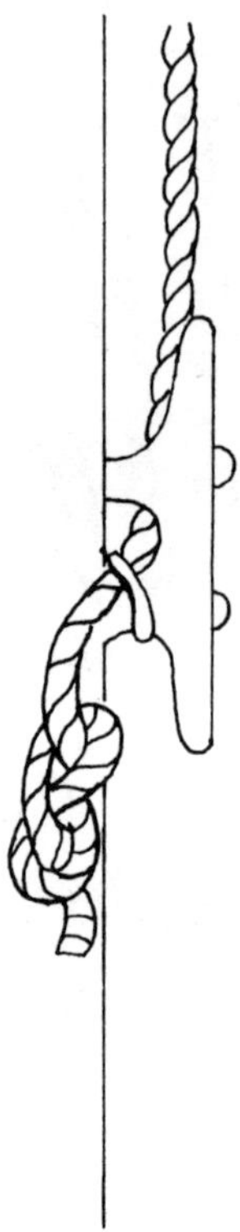

Figure 25. Figure-eight knots are the quickest stoppers to tie. All sheets and halyards should have them tied in for safety and convenience.

The key to all sail trim is simplicity. Sure, the racers have their hydraulics, grooved headstays, Barber haulers, triradials and cross-linked grinders, and if you wish to clutter up your deck and rig with these and others of the same ilk, go ahead. But you will discover that they do not increase boat speed or crew efficiency unless there is more than one of you ... and there ain't.

All boats have their peculiarities, and each one will take some sailing to get the feel of what is best in different sets of circumstances. A masthead rig will take different trim techniques than a ⅞ or ¾ rig. A ketch will take vastly different handling techniques than a sloop and so on. But the key to sail trim is to get the most out of your sails, with the least effort, for the optimum boat speed. Your progress singlehanding will be slower than that of a fully crewed yacht, but by isolating the factors that produce the greatest speed with the least continual adjustment, you'll be able to more than hold your own.

I have seen many sailors on a reach with the genny let out short of luffing and the main tight. Now, if you think about it, this causes the main to act as a brake, not to mention that any semblance of balance is destroyed and the boat becomes more than difficult to steer. Yet hundreds of sailors who actually know better let this take place. Why? The answer seems to be that they are so concerned with genoa trim and steering, and with shouting at the crew to play the foresail sheets, that as helmsmen they neglect to trim the main.

Every book on sailing has detailed technical explanations of the slot effect. What it boils down to is that when main and foresail are trimmed with a parallel curve to their respective leeches, greater aerodynamic efficiency is achieved. Can you imagine an airplane with one wing at 90 degrees to the fusilage, and the other at 45 degrees? It boggles the mind. The dynamic principles are the same: wings through air. In the case of the boat, the wing is a bit softer, but it serves exactly the same function. You won't crash if you haven't the proper trim, but you won't move very well either.

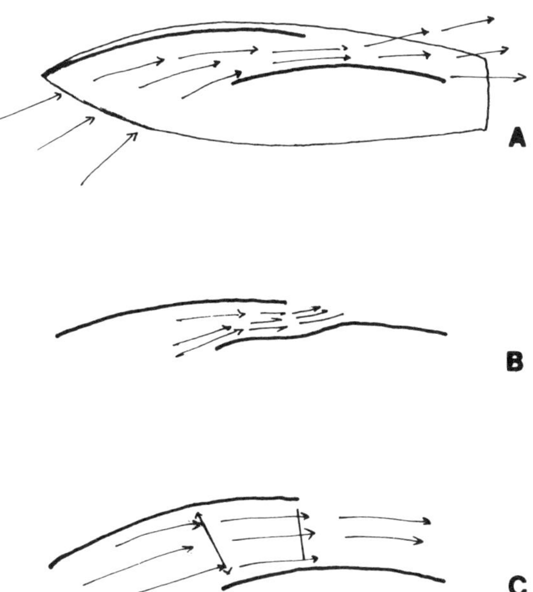

Figure 26. Slot effect. **A.** Correct. **B.** Too closed. **C.** Too open.

The simplest way to cope with the slot effect, which essentially presents the most sail to the wind, is to haul in your sails as you tack, then let them out until they start to luff, finally taking them back in so that they are just short of luffing on your new course.

You'll find this strategy effective both when beating to windward and when reaching. However, as the wind comes aft of the beam, the chances of successfully maintaining any effective slot are greatly lessened. In the first place, you may have to contend with quartering seas, which will do their damndest to spill wind from either sail, usually by knocking the boat just enough off course to either overfill or empty the sails.

Secondly, and especially in light air, the apparent wind is less downwind. You will therefore have a much harder time trimming sail with the wind aft. If it is dead astern, you have the options of sailing wing and wing or on one sail. However, since the main and jib are usually of greatly differing area, you will find it difficult to balance the boat, and steering will become more of an effort. I have found that quite often main and working jib are about the same area. Winged out, with the jib on the whisker pole and *both* sails

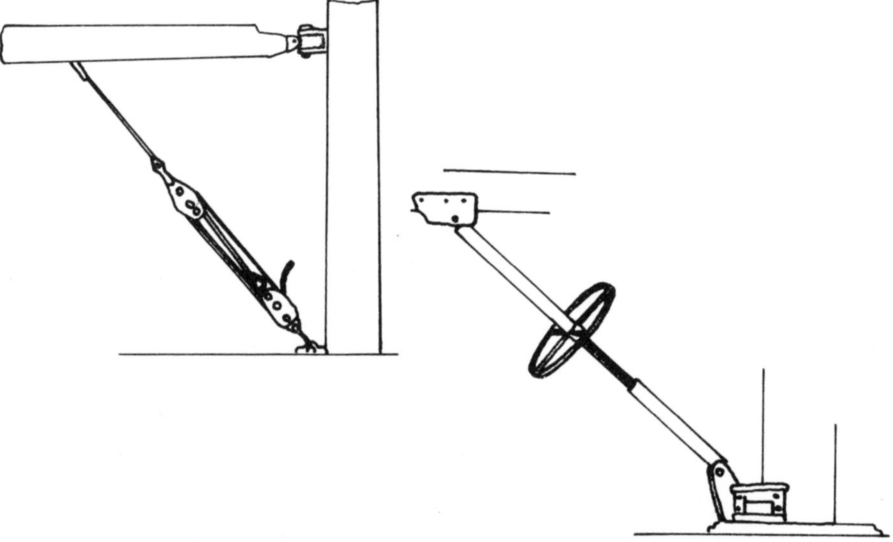

Figure 27. Boom vangs. **A.** A traditional block and tackle purchase. **B.** An adjustable solid vang. This one not only holds the boom down, it also holds the boom up.

vanged, a much more accurate course can be maintained. In a howling gale, however, I would opt for a small headsail alone. The danger of a jibe is too great and you can't cope alone with safety.

Vangs can be rigged in a number of different ways. You can take a line from the clew of the jib poled out, to a block on the foredeck or the toerail, and run it back to the cockpit. Another possibility is to run the vang line to a specially mounted clam cleat on the forward coaming. This acts as a safety release.

Mains can be vanged from boom to mast, or to the deck just aft of the mast, but this will *not* prevent a jibe. A preventer must be rigged, traditionally to the lee rail, by means of a strap and rope arrangement.

I would use a nylon line (true for the foresail vang, too) for its shock absorbing qualities, and would suggest the same arrangement I described for the jib. Namely, a block attached to the toerail, with the line run back to a clam cleat on the forward coaming. There are times when you must release vangs quickly, and this, in all likelihood, will provide the easiest way for a solo sailor to do it.

I hope you don't try to take on too much at once. Spinnakers are without doubt the best sails off the wind. If you have the strength and skill to set one alone, fine. Most sailors, especially cruising sailors, might find them daunting. The problem is not so much setting them, but dousing them. A thousand feet of snarled, billowing nylon is little fun. Also, to steer and trim a spinnaker at the same time is difficult because of the number of lines needed to efficiently manage the sail.

Most of the preceding discussion has had to do with headsails. After all, they comprise the largest part of your inventory, cost the most and demand the most attention in setting and trimming. Mains get mistreated, creased, chafed and neglected. Yet, except in the most radical of IOR boats, they are the workhorses of sailing. After all, that's why they are called "mains."

A mainsail has to be strong, capable of being handled with just a few adjustments (very few) and infinitely versatile. You have one, and it has to suffice for all the conditions under which four or five headsails might be used. When you finally break down and order a new one, here are a few things to think about when you talk to your sailmaker.

Cloth: Often a main is constructed of much heavier cloth than is necessary. First decide where you will be cruising. If it's predominantly a light air area, you can opt for a lighter sail than might be the norm. If you plan world cruising, go for one that's heavier. Modern Dacron can take almost anything (even sunlight, with the new light-stabilized cloths) and the problems that do arise have mainly to do with the stitching. If you plan any extended offshore passages, you may wish to consider a softer cloth than that used for racing. It is easier to handle, will last longer and stows in a smaller space.

Cut: Your boat has come supplied with a production main with battens. Your sailmaker has told you you'll get extra drive (and area) with battens. Everyone you know has battens. However, the only reason for using battens is to increase area, take advantage of rating rules and foul up your life. Battens break, are lost overboard, warp, tear sails and chafe the leech. No matter how well tapered and taped, how well secured in their pockets, they break and tear the sail and foul backstays.

Yet, despite all the obvious advantages, battenless, roped leeches are rarely seen, even aboard world cruisers. You may lose about ten to fifteen percent area this way, but you have a sail far easier to handle, with none of the disadvantages of a batten-filled main, and with distinct advantages.

Actually, on most modern boats, the slight loss in area will lessen weather helm. A good cruising boat has an almost neutral helm. Weather helm is useless except to an inexperienced sailor. For a singlehander under self-steering, weather helm won't cause the boat to turn up. Furthermore, you'll have less difficulty reefing, furling and, believe it or not, trimming the sail.

Battened mains, after hard use, tend to distort just forward of the batten pockets. With a roachless main, none of this occurs, and you'll find most mainsail handling a lot easier.

Many sailmakers have had little or no experience cutting such mains. Seek out a traditional cruising specialist who knows what he's doing. You may have to undertake some research on your own and books will be of little value. The best of the lot is Jeremy Howard-Williams' *Looking at Sails*, if you can find a copy.

If you have a battened main and intend to stay with it, see that it's in good order and doesn't foul the backstay. If it does, think about having it cut down slightly. Consult your sailmaker.

Workmanship: A thorny question, dependent upon the kind of sailing you plan to do. Triple stitching, leather chafe patches and

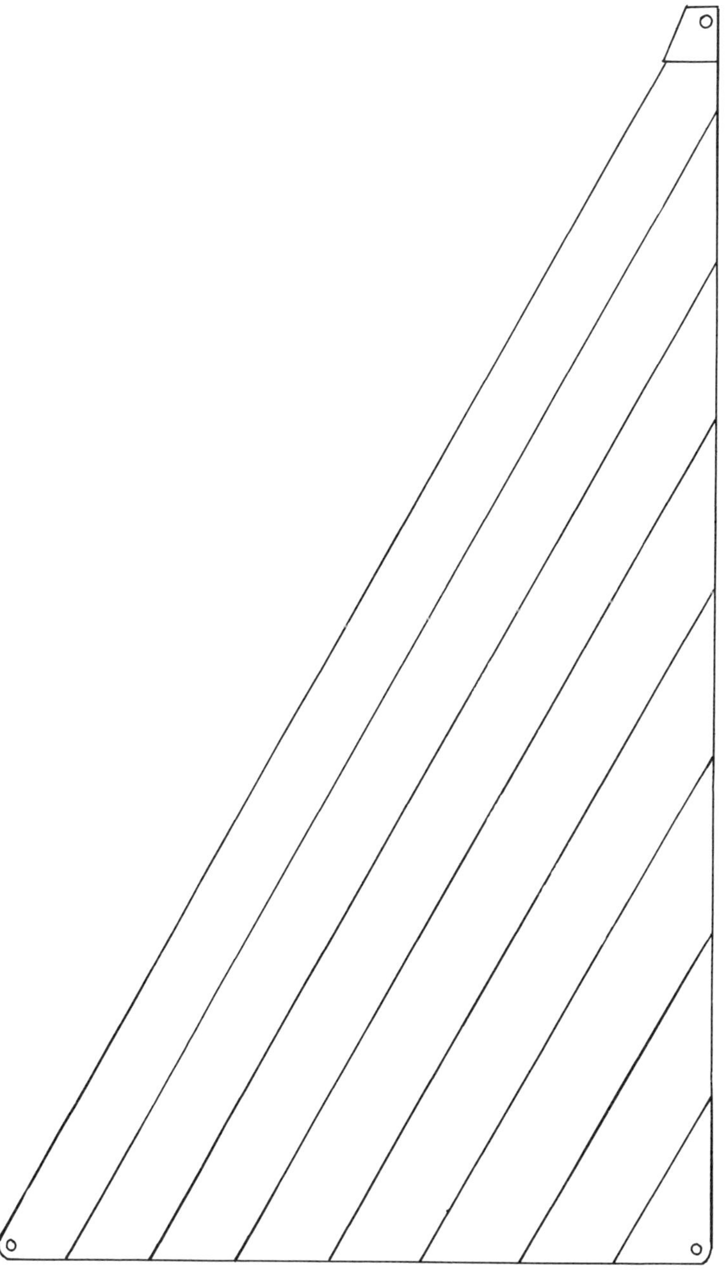

Figure 28. A battenless mainsail. Note that panels run parallel to the leech.

hand-sewn corners are all well and good for the traditionalist blue water man, but they also cost a bloody fortune. Your average cruising sail, on the other hand, is less expensive and will take an awful lot of abuse and keep on going. My own working sails (first-class to start with, needless to say) are now six years old, have been used—bagged and furled—thousands of times, cleaned once a year, never repaired and still draw beautifully.

They are double-stitched, soft Dacron cloth—nothing unusual. The headsails have never been folded except by the sailmaker, after

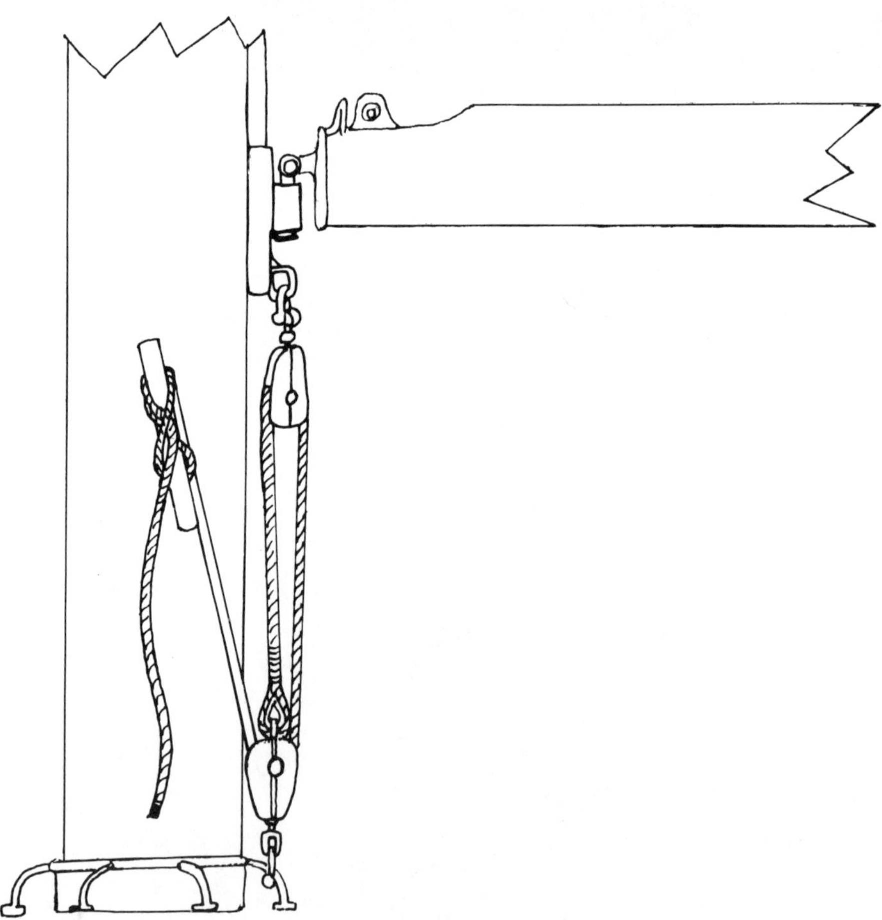

Figure 29. Downhaul. Gooseneck is track-mounted; purchase allows for simpler adjustment for draft than does fiddling with the halyard.

cleaning. The main is kept under cover on the boom. Stuffing a jib into a sail bag is frowned upon by everyone, but cruising sails aren't as critical as racing canvas, and no harm seems to be done.

Racing mains can be trimmed many ways. Draft, center of effort and fullness are adjustable. However, when you are alone you don't have time to concern yourself with these niceties, although, certain adjustments can be useful. I'm all in favor of a downhaul, though a lot of boats are fitted with fixed goosenecks. If the luff has stretched, a downhaul gives you the opportunity to firm it up without worrying about overreaching the black band and jamming the halyard sheave. A downhaul is a great help in luff adjustment when reefing, too. Whether it's a two-part, four-part or another type of system is of little matter as long as it works with minimum effort. Usually, and for a singlehander this is a necessity, it is cleated off with a cam cleat. A horned back-up cleat is a good idea for a blow.

Outhaul purchases are a mixed blessing. True, they allow greater finesse in draft positioning, but a well-cut cruising main shouldn't need much. I have noticed that the small sheave blocks and wire rope used for most outhauls can create havoc with abrasion and chafe, and a broken internal outhaul is impossible to repair at sea. A three-foot line, spliced to the clew ring and reeved through the boom end fitting a few times, works. Tie it off with two half-hitches, and you can adjust it at will.

Topping lifts are absolutely necessary in any cruising boat, and they should be of Dacron rope or vinyl-covered wire.

5
Self-steering

The most exhausting part of singlehanded sailing is sitting at the wheel or tiller for hours on end. Even if you intend to keep to coastal hops, self-steering is something you must seriously consider for passages of more than 35 miles. Yet very few boats have been equipped with self-steering devices, at least in the United States. They are far more common in England and France.

Remember, however, self-steering does not take the place of a proper lookout. It cannot avoid obstacles. It will aid in avoiding fatigue, however, and permit you to navigate coastal passages with greater comfort and safety. It must be used with discretion and never in congested or crowded areas—moorings, harbor entrances, channels and shipping lanes.

Self-steering devices fall into two broad categories: wind powered and electrically driven. Under the first heading come all wind vanes and sheet-to-tiller rigs, no matter what degree of complexity or simplicity they may attain. Under the second come all autopilots. The important thing to keep in mind when choosing a system is that wind vanes keep course to the tune of the apparent wind, while autopilots follow a compass course, no matter what.

The advantages of one over the other are dependent on the average wind strength in your usual cruising grounds, the time you'll be under power and the design and balance of your boat. An autopilot can be used with sails alone only if the wind is steady and from one quadrant. Otherwise, you will spend most of your time trimming sails, and your fatigue factor will go up. Just what you're trying to avoid.

Yet, in light wind areas, a wind vane, unless very friction-free and reasonably sophisticated (servo-pendulum), will not be able to transfer the wind strength into enough force to effectively steer the boat. Donald Hamilton, the author of the Matt Helm books, uses an autopilot on his 27-foot cutter and is very satisfied with its performance. But he also does much of his singlehanding in light air, at night and under power.

Many sailors feel they must be at the tiller when the wind pipes up. After all, isn't that the rationale for sailing? For daysailing, and with a crew, yes. But when you are alone, energy conservation is of prime importance, and you can be equally thrilled standing in the bows while the wind vane fights the tiller on its own.

Vanes usually work best when beating, since most boats can be made to balance themselves and sail a reasonably true course to windward. In any case, a vane will enhance the accuracy of the course steered. The vane will, in fact, steer a better course than you, since it is more sensitive to changes, gusts and such. Also, it is always working and will automatically correct all the errors a helmsman might make once his powers of concentration have begun to diminish. Over a long period of time, the vane will outperform Ted Turner or Paul Elvstrom.

Since the apparent wind is much less downwind, a vane will tend to be more erratic on this point of sailing. It is constantly responding to slight wind changes. Thus, downwind, where the boat's directional stability is lessened, the vane will steer from one side to the other. The true course will probably average out, but to an observer ashore, it may well look as if a slightly tipsy sailor has taken the helm.

On a reach, the gear will respond in relation to the wind speed. Heavy air will cause—again, with exceptions—more erratic behavior than moderate air. And too much sail up can cause wild gyrations. In other words, the sail power can overcome any mechanical advantage the vane would normally have.

If you sail a small boat without engine, as I do, there's really no choice. But deciding on which vane to buy is another matter. Much depends on the shape of the hull, the sail plan and the natural directional stability of the boat. Generally, long, slim hulls with the rudder aft-mounted on a substantial skeg will have greater directional stability than a fat IOR-styled underbody. Spade rudders, which have little or no place on an offshore boat, are variable in their response to the helm. Those on Ted Hood's and Bill Lapworth's boats are slightly balanced and have a vertical stock. They seem to be more responsive. The new breed of boats designed by

Holland, Peterson and Frers have enormous rudders, but are designed for massive power, which is not needed for self-steering.

Long keels will usually supply a steady helm but make the boat less maneuverable. Compromise is creeping up on us. Moderation is again the keynote. A moderate boat with moderate overhangs, reasonable draft to prevent leeway, and a large rudder seems to be the best all around solution. This assumes you'll use the boat for daysailing, coastal hops, occasional races and offshore passages. No boat is ideal, but the more traditional boat will do more of these tasks better. By traditional I don't mean some bogged-down, turn-of-the-century pilot boat, but something more like the CCA boats of the 60s and early 70s.

In any case, the moderate boat will demand less of a self-steering vane than some out-and-out racing machine. Less demand

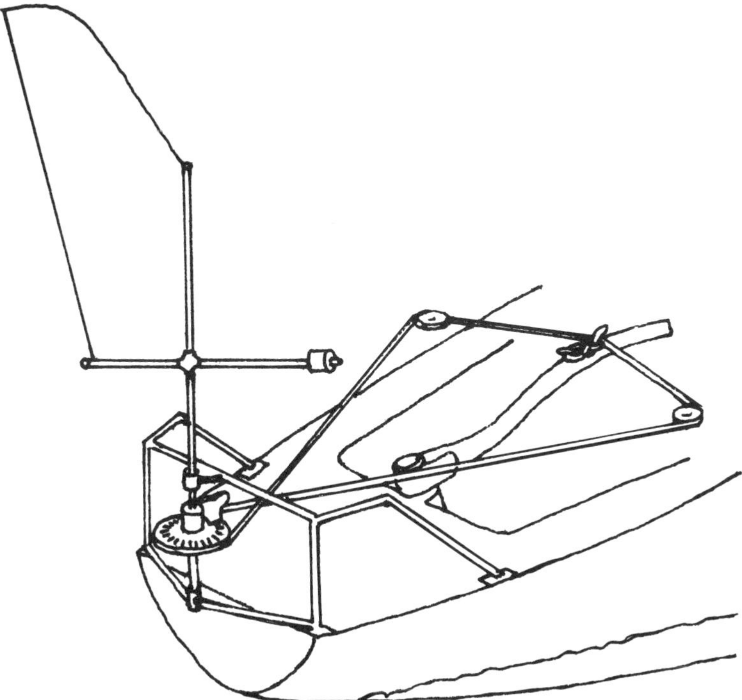

Figure 30. Simple vane-to-tiller steering gear. Suitable only for small, well-balanced boats. Coupling is directly to the tiller by means of a line turned round a vane drum.

means less expense. Small cruisers with decent lateral plane can get by on a vane-to-tiller set-up. Whether the vane is pivoted vertically or horizontally is a matter of choice, though the horizonal vane will generally exert greater power. With this system, bearings and pivots must be as friction-free as possible, and the tiller lines as taut as possible. The newer nonstretch Dacron for halyards works well. Assuming there is no mizzen to contend with, the vane is best mounted as high and as far aft as possible.

If you happen to have a transom-hung rudder and you wish a greater range of self-steering abilities, trim tab system may be the answer. Developed by "Blondie" Hasler, the OSTAR originator, this form of vane apparatus works by having the vane actuate a small trim tab attached to the trailing edge of the rudder. When the vane

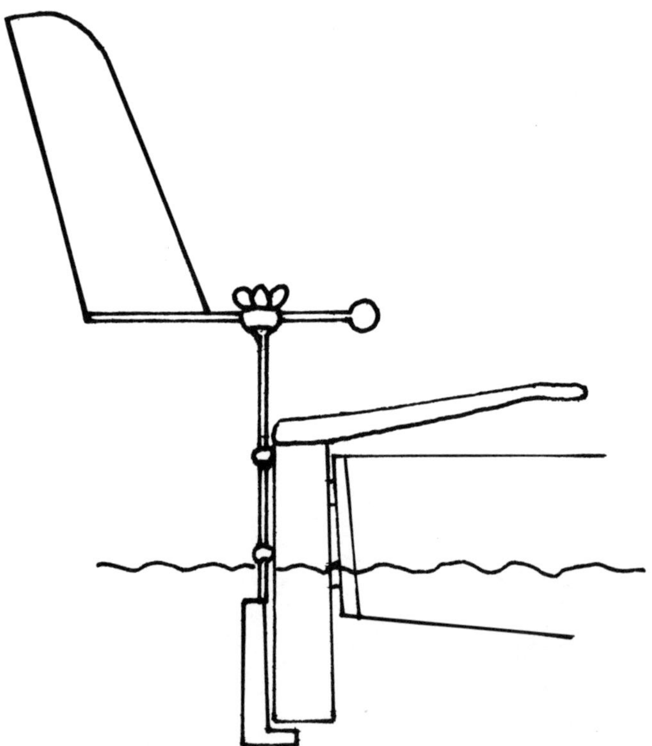

Figure 31. Trimtab to vane gear. Vane directly moves a trim tab attached to the rudder. Water pressure on the trim tab provides the force necessary to in turn initiate rudder movement.

is turned by a change in wind direction, it turns the trim tab through a linkage system, which in turn causes the rudder to swing and correct course.

Beyond these, vanes quickly become more expensive and more complicated, and if your boat is in the 35-foot-and-over range, you will have to opt for one of these more sophisticated systems. The vane-to-tiller set-up hasn't the power, and you won't find many transom-hung rudders on larger boats.

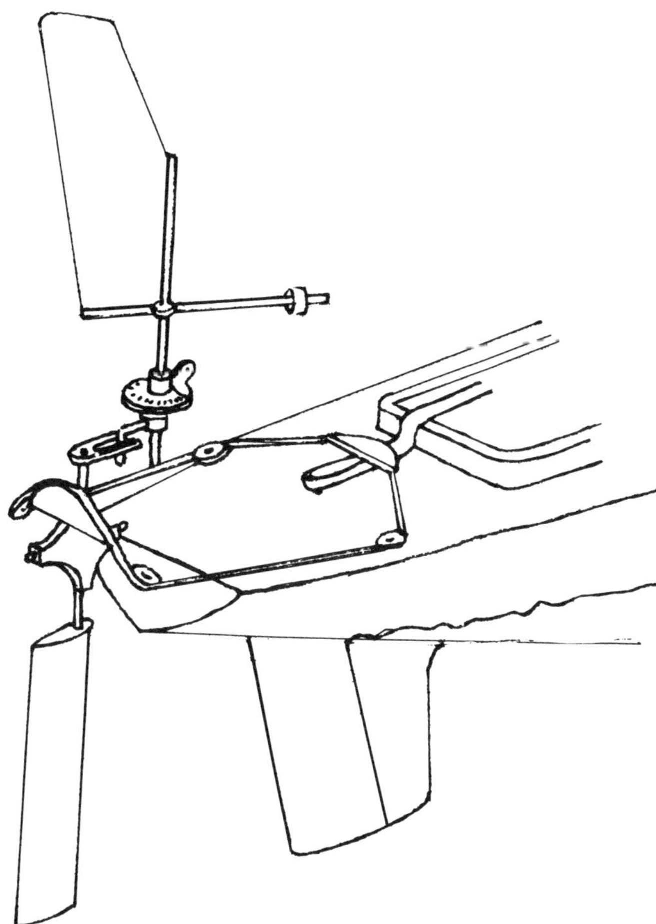

Figure 32. Pendulum vane steering gear. The vane, through a linkage, moves the deep underwater blade. Water pressure on the blade causes the entire assembly to pivot about the horizontal axis (pendulum effect) accentuating the pull on the tiller lines.

The answer in such cases is a pendulum vane gear. Here the trim tab is actually an independent pendulum in the water and turns on both horizontal and vertical axes. Thus it will be forced by the pressure of the water to assume the same position as the centerline of the boat and will turn vertically at the same time to actuate the helm via tiller lines.

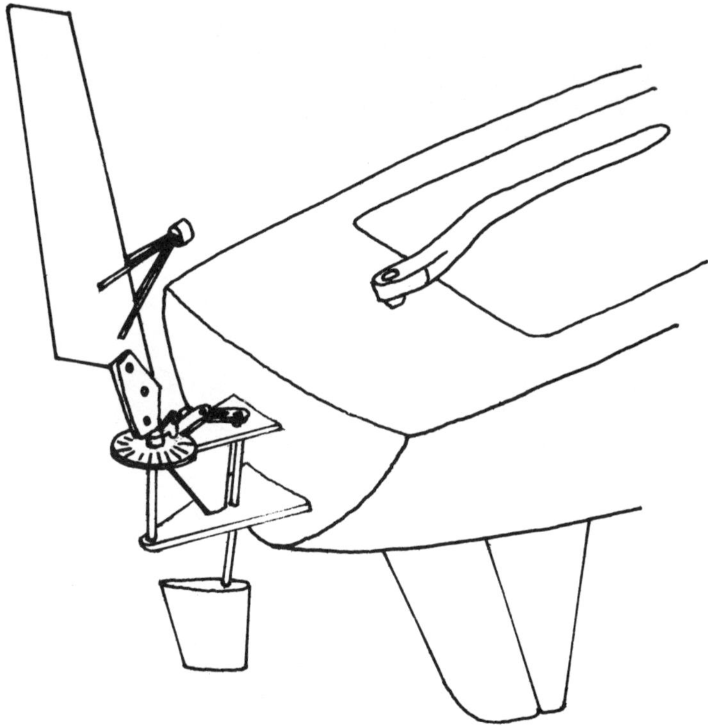

Figure 33. Direct vane to auxiliary rudder steering gear. Boat's rudder can be set to correct balance and helm.

Variations exist, some with their own auxiliary rudders, some with adjustable linkages, some with horizontal or vertical vanes, some with smaller vanes, and so on. The principles are all the same, and in choosing a vane gear you must take into account the boat's performance as well as its general handling characteristics. Gerard Dijkstra's excellent little book *Self-Steering for Sailboats* is the best general guide to the subject, though John Letcher's *Self-Steering for Sailing Craft* is more complete but also more technical.

You will have to experiment to some degree. I know of only two vane gear manufacturers who essentially custom build vanes for particular boats. Otherwise, you buy off the shelf.

Remember, your choice must be dictated by the sailing characteristics, hull type and sail plan of your ship. If you have money to burn, units like the Mustafa or Sailomat will steer almost anything, but their cost is well over $2000. Some of the smaller vanes, especially the French Navik, are reasonable in cost, light and reliable. If you have a wheel, you will have to make or buy a drum attachment to allow the tiller lines to work (or get an auxiliary rudder set-up).

A final possibility is sheet-to-tiller rigs. A great deal of trial-and-error experimentation is necessary, however, to get them to work. The diagrams show the most common arrangements. Since the cost is minimal, they are well worth a try before investing in a vane or autopilot.

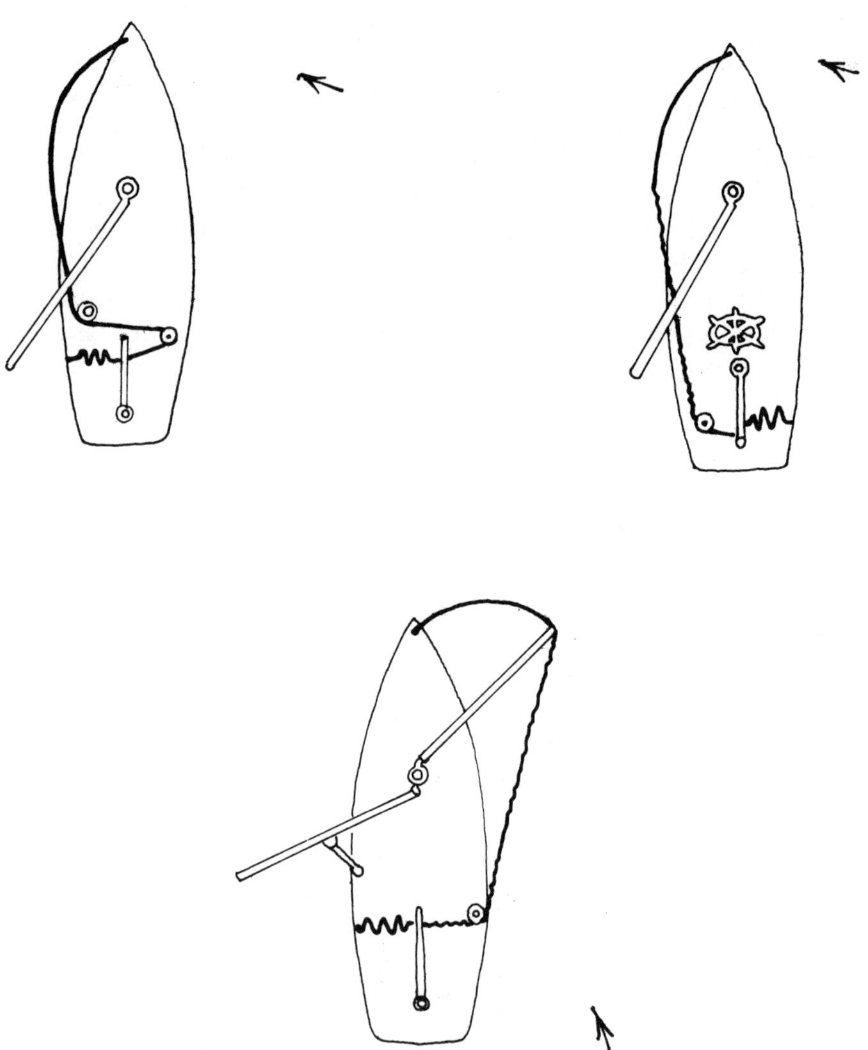

Figure 34. Sheet-to-tiller rigs. (After Henderson). Upper Left: Jib sheet passes about winches as shown. Force is counterpoised by a length of shockcord to leeward. Upper right: With a wheel steering system, the emergency tiller can be used to accomplish the same effect, except that with tiller in verso, shock cord hooks up to windward. Bottom: Running with poled-out jib. All these methods of steering demand much experimentation, depending on boat type and rig. See John Letcher, *Self-Steering for Sailing Craft*, International Marine Publishing Company, 1974).

6
Planning and the Avoidance of Fatigue

The greatest enemy of the solo sailor is fatigue. No ifs, ands or buts. Tiredness causes unclear thinking, which in turn leads to unbelievable stupidity. Even in experienced sailors. I remember once sailing to Nantucket from City Island. The seas were lumpy, it was cold, I had been on watch for more than 14 hours. Not only was my navigation off—I was five miles too far to the south—but I had started to imagine I was sailing uphill. I decided to put into Menemsha Pond and was promptly rammed against the pier by the currents running inside the entrance. So much for my seamanship!

On an offshore passage, sleep is possible, when far enough away from shipping lanes, lee shores and navigational hazards. But in confined waters, and at any distance less than 50 miles or so from land, a constant watch must be kept, not only of the boat and its components, but of *everything* around. Water, sky, buoys, ships, landmarks. And that watch must be constant and of second nature. Actually, the human mind is ill-suited for concentration aboard a yacht, unless trained for just that task. Every time you introduce a new crew member to the dubious joys of sailing, he or she is given a turn at the helm. The percentage of "concentrators" who can keep a course for more than a minute or two is very low. They look at the gulls, at other boats, at the topless beauty on the big ketch. But can they keep their minds plastered on sails and wind shifts? Not easily, unless they have grasped the fact that much more important matters are at hand (and eye). You may have been sailing for 20 years and never have been in the position of having to understand the magnitude or multiplicity of tasks involved in sailing because others have taken responsibility for them.

Fatigue is not merely due to standing watch. It can arise from a complex combination of factors. Steady sun, heavy meals and booze, combined with the routine tasks aboard any yacht, are enough to cause most any sailor to feel tired and draggy and to lose the concentration and reflexes needed to make sharp and fast judgments.

How do you prevent fatigue? And what can you do about it once it's come on? The answer to both questions is simple . . . sleep. However, there are times when sleep is the one thing you cannot do, no matter what.

It helps to start a sail fresh. If you plan to start at dusk—something to be recommended, since you can then make port during daylight—sleep the day before. Stay up the preceding night if necessary, but try not to be up for more than a few hours before casting off.

As the body wakes up, it burns energy at an astonishing rate, especially when engaged in strenuous tasks. If possible, have everything aboard and set to take off the day before you plan to leave. Rest your muscles as well as your brain. Have a hearty, but not rich, meal at least three hours before you board your boat. Keep fruits and crackers handy to the helm for your first nourishment on board. Most important, eat when hungry, not when you feel you *should*. Keeping a constant level of food-supplied energy and blood sugar is important for continuing physical and mental effectiveness.

Don't drink alcohol. Don't drink carbonated beverages. Don't eat greasy or heavily sugared foods. Not initially, at any rate. Try to eat a lot of roughage—greens, lettuce, bran and such. The change of environment and habit is likely to cause constipation, which will not only cause discomfort but will add to the fatigue problem. Get your sea legs before plunging into that pot of five alarm chili. Moderation is the rule. Of course, there are always exceptions but, by and large, what you eat will have a great effect on your reactions, alertness and general ability to stay awake.

Excessive amounts of coffee will *not* keep you alert. It may keep you up, but the tension it produces, added to your existing anxiety over the impending voyage will probably cause rushed actions, erratic behavior and ill-considered judgments.

Likewise, no drugs of any kind (unless necessary for health

maintenance) should be taken before or during sailing. Barbiturates and amphetamines are bad enough on land. Alone at sea, you are literally taking your life into your hands by disrupting an already ajar system and putting undue strain on your heart. Barbiturates and amphetamines impair ability to make rational decisions. The same goes for marijuana and cocaine or other narcotics. You may feel increased sensitivity and heightened perceptions, but it just ain't so. I know of one crew member, stoned on grass, who conned a 39-footer into Vineyard Haven under full sail. She claims that her one reaction afterwards was overwhelming terror. And, the boat and crew (all equally done in) were an absolute menace to the many other boats maneuvering in the harbor. Unless you want to take the chance of killing yourself or someone else, stay off anything that might alter your normal consciousness.

Underway, the greatest threat to staying awake is standing the helm. Sure, it's fun and exciting to steer your ship through wind and waves. It is also tiring. Something like driving a car for 10 hours. If you have fitted self-steering or can rig a sheet-to-tiller rig, use it whenever you're not in congested waters. On most points of sail—depending on your boat—such an arrangement will steer a truer course than you can. By not expending the energy needed to concentrate, you'll manage to stay far more alert and will be better able to protect yourself from the elements.

Cold, wet—*tired.* The converse is true. Warm, dry—*alert.* How do you best stay that way? Most experts agree on two dressing procedures: first, wear layers of relatively light clothing; second, wear natural fibers, particularly cotton and wool. Also, fitting a protective dodger will help, especially when beating.

Even in hot sunny weather, it's a good idea to wear loose fitting shirts and pants. Prolonged exposure to the sun's rays produces not only a bad burn, but drowsiness, thirst and general lassitude. Cotton is best. It is soft, light and porous. Perspiration will evaporate faster than with any synthetics, leaving you cooler and more refreshed.

When it starts to get cold, and especially at night, it's time to cover up. Start with cotton underwear and a cotton flannel shirt, topped with a wool sweater. Wool is a remarkable thing; even wet it functions to retain body heat. I prefer baggy corduroys below the belt. Jeans are tough, sure, but they are tight and can bind. You are going to have to move around the deck, and you might as well be able to do it with freedom. Full-cut corduroy trousers fit the bill. If

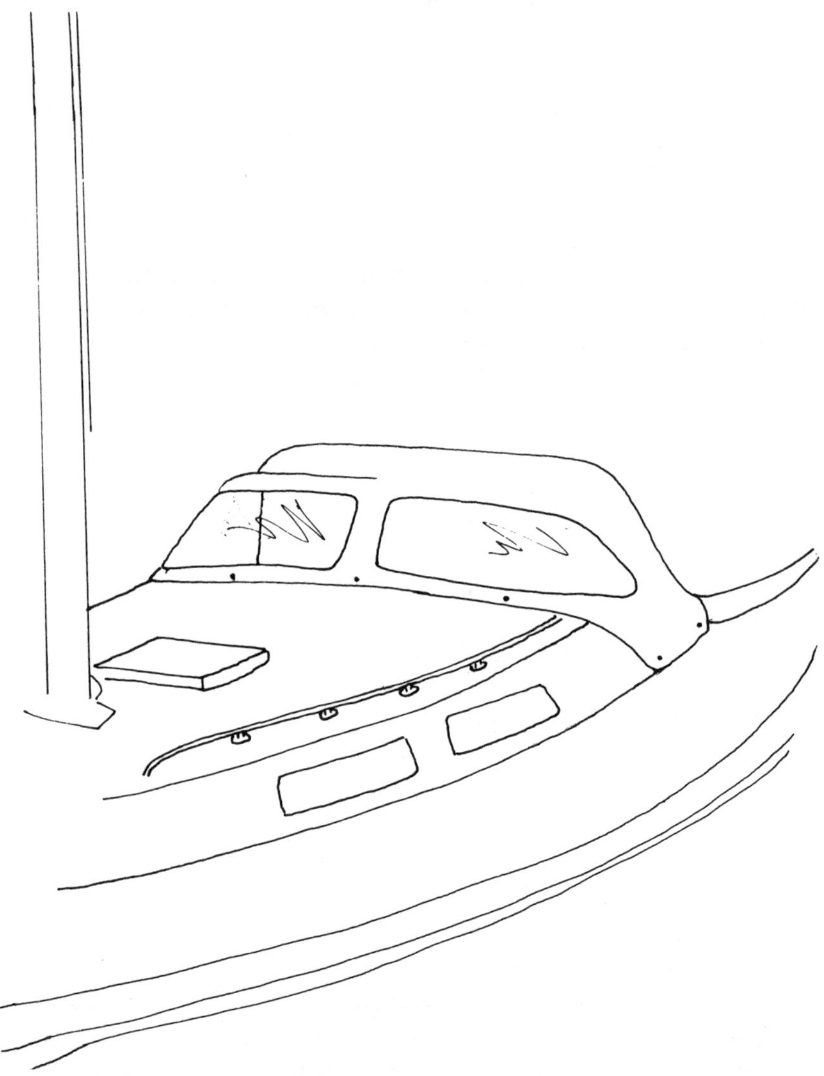

Figure 35: Cockpit dodger. Of invaluable use for protection from wind and spray. Crouching behind keeps you alert and dry. Most sailmakers will custom fit one to your boat.

it gets colder still, add foul weather gear, chest high pants first. Sitting on a cold deck will make you lose more body heat from your rump than you lose from uncovered shoulders.

Whether your foul weather jacket is hooded or not is a matter of personal preference. Some sailors prefer a sou'wester. I like the hood, with a battered old tennis hat underneath or, in cold weather, a wool watch cap. Feet and hands, along with the head, are the points of greatest body heat loss. A light pair of cotton socks with wool ones over them and a good pair of large deck boots complete this fashionable outfit.

The thing to remember is to be comfortable—and cautious. If a storm is impending, dress beforehand. It's no use trying to get into oilies when your clothes are wet.

Assuming you're warm, dry and well-fed, what else can you do to stay fresh? Learn to pace yourself. For example, in going forward to change a headsail, don't rush around, tripping over things, running back and forth between cockpit and foredeck. *Before* you go forward, take stock of the situation. What will you need? Sail bag, new sail, knife, sail ties, safety harness (if it's nighttime, you should have this on anyway). Organize all these on and about your person, clip on the harness and proceed *slowly* along the weather deck.

Okay, you've arrived at the bows. Tie the new sail bag to the pulpit and hank the new headsail onto the forestay below the still-drawing sail. Now, depending on your set-up, you've got choices. This is one reason I prefer the halyards to terminate at the mast, not the cockpit. You have only half the distance to go. Move back to the mast, slack off the jib halyard and go forward to haul down the jib. You could let the boat luff slightly during this process, since there's no one to steer things aft. Bag the jib before you do anything else, and secure it to the rail. Attach the sheets to the new sail, then the halyard. Taking the old sail with you (or stuffing it down the forehatch), move back to the mast and haul up the new sail. Go back to the cockpit, put the boat on course and trim. It's done.

Another possibility is to heave-to for this task, but certain requirements must be met by both boat and rig for this to work. See the heavy weather section for details.

Try to pace yourself with everything. The best way, probably, is to draw up a series of activity plans. For each task—sail changing, anchoring, cooking, tacking and so on—sit down and actually work out exactly what you plan to do, in what order, under varying conditions.

It demands method and patience to make up list after list, step by step. You'll learn a lot in the process, too. One, that you know more than you think you do. Two, that you can probably streamline and better organize some of your activities. And that could mean greater efficiency at sea, less strain and less fatigue, not to mention greatly reduced anxiety.

7
Standing Watch and Watching Out

The 1972 COLREGS (International Regulations for Avoiding Collision at Sea) are quite explicit: all ships must post a lookout at all times. The fact that many don't and that the seas of the world are filled with wrecks should be warning enough to any sailor. If you are sailing alone, you can duck below for a few moments to get food, plot position and such, but your visible horizon must be clear of traffic even for that.

Some singlehanders develop a knack for sleeping an hour at a time. Some can sleep normal hours, especially in seldom traveled areas. But in coastal passages, there is little advice I can offer that will allow you to keep to the letter *and* spirit of the law as well as permit you to sleep.

Modern boats do not heave-to well, so you will either have to stay awake or else anchor for the night. The risks are too great to suggest anything else. I have seen fully crewed boats run down by a long tow in broad daylight on a clear day. Inattention was the cause. When you're alone, the chances of being hit are multiplied so many times that no bookmaker would place odds.

Assuming you plan to stay awake for the duration of the passage, what can be done to make sure you don't get run down? The best advice I know was published in the May, 1980 issue of *Cruising World*. The article "Can They See You From Up There?" by Rick Butler, a U.S. Navy Commander and very experienced big ship driver, suggests the following (amended and simplified by me):

1. Install a masthead-mounted strobe light.
2. See if your sails can have foil-coated headboards installed

and, if you have a vane, install aluminum-covered Mylar film on the vane itself.

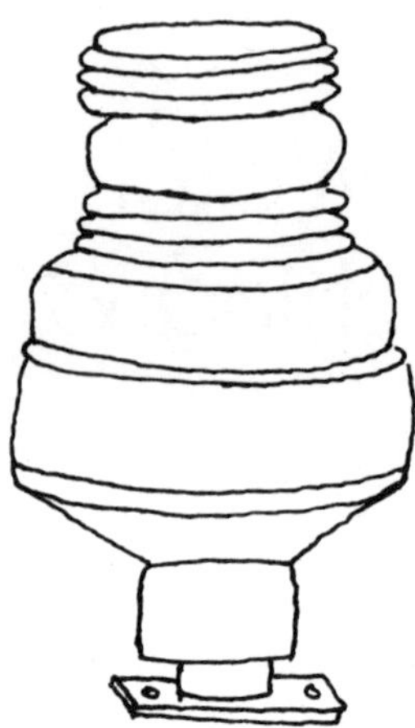

Figure 36. Masthead strobe light. No other light is as bright, or can be seen for such a great distance. A superb emergency signal.

3. Offshore, consider tanbark colored sails. White doesn't show up well from a distance.
4. If you can't do the masthead strobe number, use a man-overboard strobe for signaling your position.
5. Have a big spotlight aboard. Aim at the oncoming ship, not your sails.
6. As soon as you can guess his course, steer away from his track. Don't wait! Modern ships move a sea mile every two minutes.
7. Never use flares to identify yourself. They may attract would-be rescuers who could run you down.
8. Most standard pleasure boat navigation lights cannot be seen readily. Get big ones and mount them as high as possible. The ideal solution is a tricolor masthead light combined with your strobe. Red and green running lights should be mounted on the pulpit, not the deckhouse or cabin. Sails will obscure them.
9. Always assume the ship will NOT see you.
10. Forget the fact that ships are supposed to stay to regular lanes. On the open oceans, ships today use Optimum Track Ships Routing (OTSR) and stray far from those pilot chart tracks.

Also, the old rule "sail has the right of way" can be thoroughly

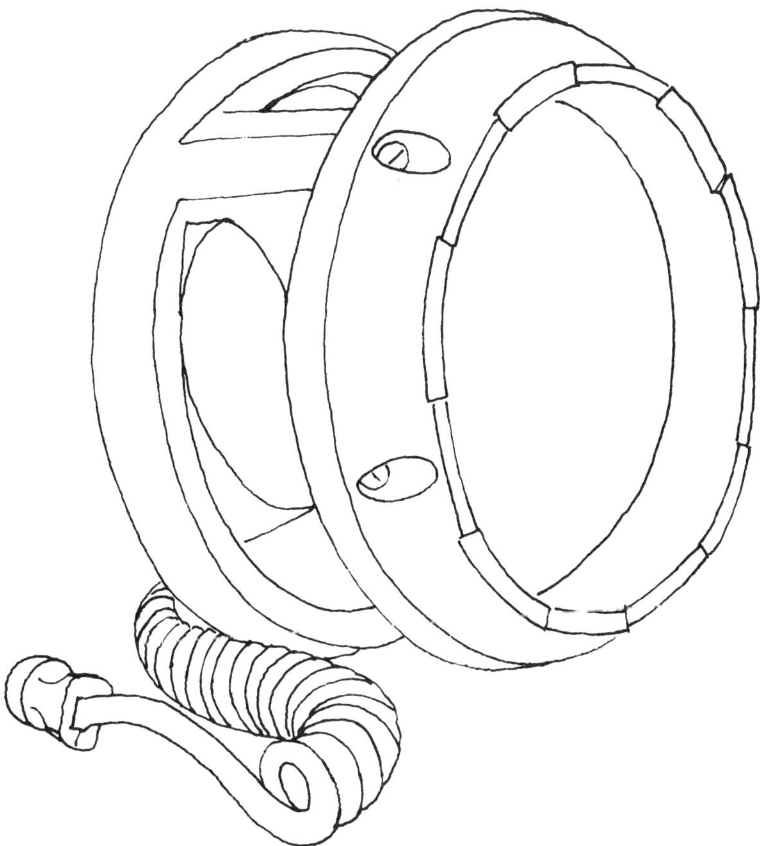

Figure 37. Self-contained, battery powered lights have neither the power nor the penetration of a spotlight wired into the main electrical system. A deck plug makes for easy stowage and quick access.

discounted. If you are aboard a 300-foot long, full-rigged ship, maybe. Otherwise, run like hell!

The above may keep ships from running you down, but they won't help you avoid stationary obstructions that happen to be in your path. Currents, wind shifts and compass deviation can have a disastrous effect on your course. You must know where you are, certainly a function of the most basic navigation. Nevertheless, experienced sailors have found themselves thrown 30 or more miles off course by adverse currents, beer cans next to the binnacle (and batteries in flashlights too) or wind shifts in the middle of the night.

A safe rule to follow is that when you're nearer to shore than 50 miles, stay awake, and stay in the cockpit or wheelhouse. Further out—except in port approaches such as Boston Harbor, San Francisco Bay, anything along the southern coast of England, off Durban, and so on—a certain amount of sleep is a safer bet, but you can never be sure when a ship will come over the horizon and "discover" you.

Although I have not used them, off-course alarms and radar detectors may help. Off-course alarms are activated by a sensor compass, set to ring when a course is surpassed either side by 10

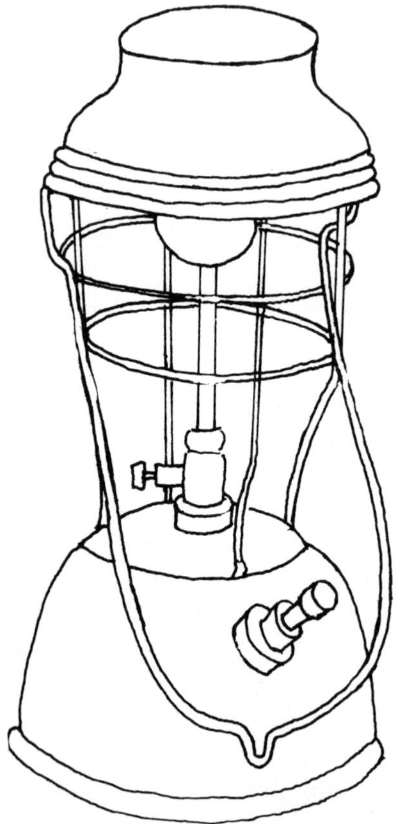

Figure 38. A storm lantern. The best readily available are the Tilley lanterns from Ireland. Not cheap, but the pressure kerosene mantle is brighter and more reliable than the so-called "storm lanterns" manufactured in the Far East.

degrees or so. They have been used with varying degrees of success. They are expensive and, like all electronics, they are subject to corrosion and malfunctioning. But they are certainly worth a try if you sail offshore with any regularity.

Radar detectors are simpler and cheaper. An alarm is activated when a signal is received from big ship radar. Since signals vary, set the alarm for several ranges, say 8, 16, 32 and 48 miles. A minimum range of 8 miles will allow you to take evasive action and maneuver away from the potential dangers.

Nevertheless, none of these devices or visual aids will substitute for a properly kept watch, scanning the horizon—360 degrees—every 10 minutes at the absolute minimum. Singlehanding is best for a short coastal passage or a long haul. The intermediate voyages of two to four or five days are potentially the most dangerous and demand the greatest care and planning of all.

8
Safety

Safety considerations for the singlehander are not much different from those aboard the fully crewed yacht. The differences lie mainly in the deployment of materials and devices, and in the added precautions that must be taken. The primary consideration, especially if the boat is fitted with a self-steering device, is staying in the boat.

To that end, lifelines should be installed. Stanchions must be at least 24 inches high, preferably 27 or even 30. Lifelines are effective only if you don't pitch over them or under them. Double or triple lines are called for in any serious passage undertaken alone. Made of wire, coated or not, or of Dacron rope (less painful and cheaper), they should be fitted with toggles or end fittings that allow adjustment and fatigue-free movement. Gates are a problem. Although they are convenient, they are the weak link in the chain, since a number of pelican hooks on the market are cheaply manufactured in the Far East. If you are agile enough to singlehand, you can probably do with clambering over lifelines. Pulpit and stern rail must be strong and also high. Too often they are designed to keep sails and cushions from going over, and not 200 pounds of accelerating humanity. The force of a body thrown across a deck is awesome and capable of ripping out rails.

Second, you must always wear a safety harness at night and in anything over a force 4–5. I know singlehanders who don't, and I hope their families survive their grief and enjoy the insurance. Be confident, but don't be foolish! The type of harness to wear is a touchy question. In Great Britain, a standard exists for "proofed" harnesses. In America, you have to trust the maker. Try for something with two-inch webbing, welded, triple-stitched, with stainless steel rings and fasteners. The line should be braided Dacron or

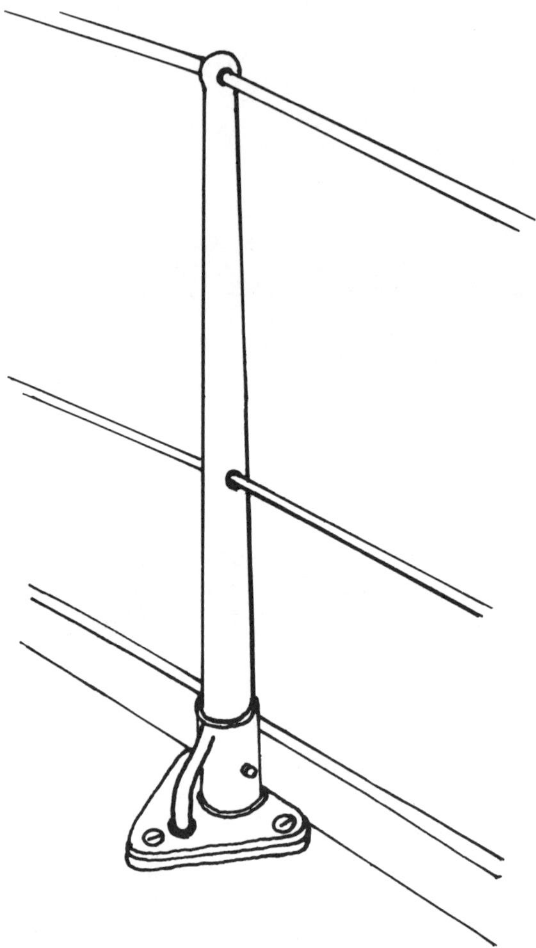

Figure 39. Proper lifelines and stanchions. Lifelines that are well braced, of heavy stock, 27 to 30 inches in height, with an intermediate lower are the basic safety gear aboard any boat. Make sure they are through-bolted and can really take a body thrown against them.

nylon (which absorbs more of a sudden shock) at least 7⁄16 of an inch in diameter. It should be spliced to the harness ring, terminating in an eye-spliced snap hook of some sort. I say "some sort" because the most tested hooks are probably the type used by mountain climbers. Some marine hooks have been known to bend, twist, jam and fail. Not a pleasant thought. Some harness lines are equipped with two hooks on one line. I prefer two separate lines, each about six feet long. This arrangement allows you to hook up the second before you unhook the first.

What do you attach your harness lines to? The best arrangement I know of, and the one I use, is two wire jacklines run from the cockpit to the foredeck, as close to the centerline as possible. These must be attached at either end to strong, through-bolted pad eyes by either Norseman terminals or swaged-end fittings. Toggles are a good idea to lessen twisting strains.

Be sure to hook on before you come out of the companionway. Too often, sailors have been swept out of a cockpit. Try not to clip

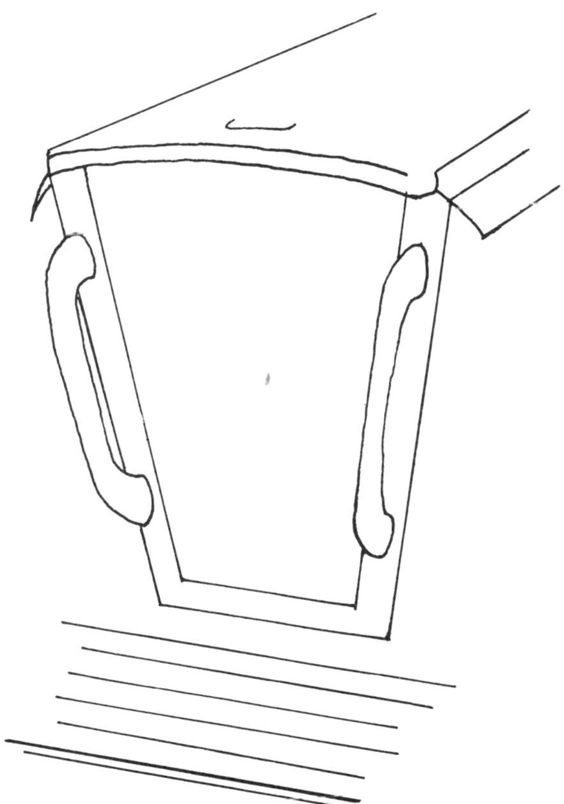

Figure 40. Handrails, and plenty of them, should be attached at strategic points on deck and below. Handholds outside and inside the companionway can easily save a life.

on to the lifelines. They will tend to act as a fulcrum to flip you overboard, whereas a centerline connection makes the lifelines into a body stop. Also, the jacklines allow for unimpeded movement fore and aft.

A float coat is a good idea at night, and there are some oilskin jackets fitted with internal harnesses, particularly those made by Henri-Lloyd and Atlantis. I find life jackets extremely constricting, but you ought to keep one handy. If the Coast Guard ever gets around to approving the inflating type, very popular in Europe, people might be more willing to wear them.

The actual surface of the deck is usually overlooked. Most of the molded-in, non-skid types are pathetic, except for collecting dirt. Non-skid paint is better, and teak is best of all, if you can afford it. Be sure that angled surfaces—the fore end of the cabin top, coamings, cockpit seats—are covered. Attractiveness must play second fiddle to safety.

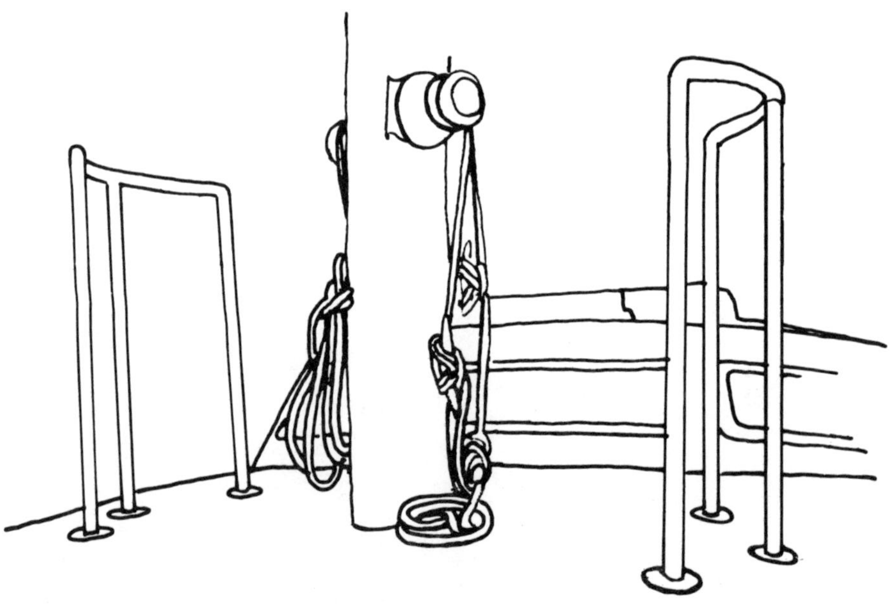

Figure 41. A larger yacht will have room on deck or cabin top for safety rails either side of the mast. These allow for two-handed work with halyards and reefing without the constant worry of body bracing against handrails or shrouds.

Cabin tops and deck houses should be equipped with plenty of through-bolted handrails made of wood and unvarnished. Besides being a pain to keep up, varnished wood is slippery enough to foil the basic purpose of a handrail.

No matter what, always go forward on the weather side of the boat. In a sudden lurch you won't be thrown over. In larger boats, safety pulpits on either side of the mast can be a boon in heavy weather.

What happens if you go overboard? Assuming your harness holds, you've got to get back on board. Unless you're a professional athlete, you will *not* be able to haul yourself over the rail, especially if the boat is moving at anything over three knots. You have suddenly added 40 to 60 pounds of water, plus the unbelievable drag of your body through the sea. Some sort of ladder is a must. For a single-hander there are really only two choices: a permanently mounted stern ladder or a quick-release emergency boarding ladder. The stern-mounted construction can be of several varieties: reaching below the waterline, folding down (in which case, a lanyard dangling to the water to lower it should be installed) or, if your ship is fitted with a transom-hung rudder, a series of steps, starting below the waterline and bolted to the rudder blade. Quick-release ladders are usually made of PVC runged rope, rolled up, with a lanyard dangling over the side. You attach them to the deck or stern rail and pull. With luck, they'll unfold.

A trailing line is most important. Generally, the best choice is polypropylene, which floats, with a bouyant ring secured to the trailing end. My experience has been that one about 75 feet long is adequate. You'd be surprised how fast the boat can get ahead of you when you pitch overboard.

Richard Henderson, in his excellent book *Singlehanded Sailing*, describes a method for attaching the trailing line to the self-steering tiller lines by means of a snap shackle. You fall over, grab the ring and the self-steering is tripped, causing the boat to round up. A thoughtful and worthwhile idea. Even with crew aboard, this isn't a bad practice. By the time they get on deck, you might well be lost in the waves. In fact, the trip line could probably be doubled, so as to also release the horseshoe and man-overboard pole, and activate a warning light below. Anything to increase safety is prudent.

For any boat going offshore, an inspected life raft is a must. They are expensive to buy and expensive to service, but they can

Figure 42. Trip line attachment for self-steering gear. The snap shackle is attached to one of the tiller steering lines. The plunger of the shackle becomes the attachment point for a line trailed overboard.

be your only lifesaving device if the boat has the temerity to sink under you. Buy the best and rig it so it will float clear of the deck or cockpit when it must. Don't put it in a locker. A waterproof duffel filled with extras not included in the raft survival pack should be lashed near the companionway. This can be packed with extra water, space blankets, food supplements, navigational tools and charts, a handbearing compass and repair materials for the raft. Don't forget writing materials and a jar of vaseline (for salt water sores). Allow a pint of water per day.

When you buy your raft, consider double floors and a ballast chamber. The Fastnet disaster has shown that, in certain conditions, standard rafts are less than life saving. Givens, Avon, Beufort, Dunlop, RDF, Surviva and Zodiac all make good rafts. Just remember, you get only what you pay for. One afterthought: the raft will be better off (and you will too) if it's a cannister pack. Valises, though handier to stow, are more susceptible to corrosion of the inflating valves.

Parachute flares should be part and parcel of the raft or boat. Very or flare pistols can corrode, so the self-contained, high power flares are probably the best. These cost between twenty and thirty dollars each and have a three year shelf life. Check the date. At least half a dozen are mandatory for both boat and raft, so keep the checkbook handy. And learn how to use them beforehand. Reading directions in the dark aboard a sinking ship is not easy.

A permanently mounted radar reflector is a necessary safety measure. Masthead reflectors are a nuisance, although they are the most effective. I carry mine wired to the backstay, twenty feet up. For the correct way to rig one, see the diagram below.

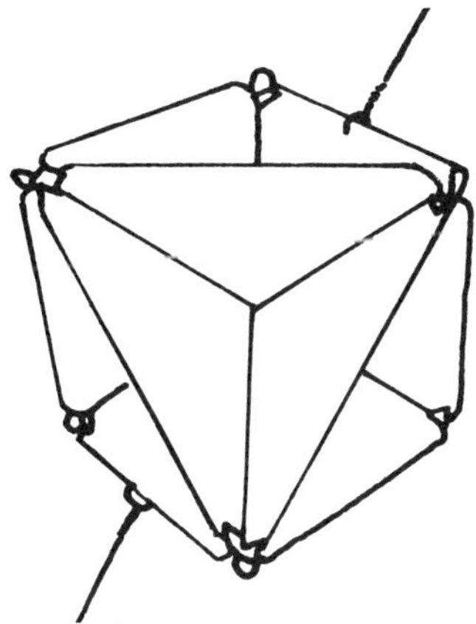

Figure 43. Radar reflectors are usually incorrectly hung. They should be in the "raincatcher" position as shown. The larger the better, with the minimum being 12 inches in diameter, with positive plate-to-plate contacts.

Providing access to the masthead is vital, and mast steps are to be recommended on anything over thirty feet. The alternative is a bosun's chair, the best of which are made of cloth, with safety straps. Be sure to rig a line that runs from the chair around the mast and is secured again to the chair. Keeps you from flying.

Bilge pumps are as important as engines. Have two manual pumps—one operable from the cockpit through a watertight gland, one inside the cabin. Despite the standard, I feel both should be capable of disposing of at least 25 gallons per minute. Anything less is for pumping out rainwater. Henderson, Whale and Edson make the best.

The above are just the basics. Unfortunately, the rest can be learned only through experience, plus a lot of talking and listening to sailors, not dockside kibitzers.

9
Heavy Weather

Sooner or later you will be caught out in heavy weather—a passing squall or a full gale offshore. You must be prepared physically, mentally and technically. You may think a squall is bad news, but wait until you have a storm at sea, with horizontal rain, 30- to 50-knot winds, and 20- or 30-foot seas. Your experiences with small storms can be, and must be, training for handling your ship with greater assurance and courage when you are faced with serious and dangerous weather conditions.

The old adage that to windward a boat can stand more than a man, and offwind a man can stand more than a boat, has great truth in it. Fighting a gale is exhausting, wet, stomach-churning work. Unless you must claw off a lee shore, run for it. Usually boat speed is so great downwind, even with no sail, that sometimes it is necessary to slow down just to survive. Survival is a matter of keeping boat and sea in rhythm. This is much easier in open waters offshore than in proximity to the continental shelf. Monster rollers can be better "danced with" than the steep coastal chop of breakers near shore.

How you go about "dancing" is another matter, depending on hull shape, rig, lateral plane, displacement and a number of other factors. But you must move with the sea, not against it. Its power is very real and very frightening. I have seen, on a transatlantic crossing, a force 10 turn stainless steel stanchions and a Hasler vane gear into spaghetti. A 20-foot wave coming down on the deck, backed by several hundred miles of sweep and the acceleration of wind and gravity, can break a Lloyds-approved boat in half. And a freak wave can do worse—witness the tragedy that befell *Morning Cloud* on her delivery trip in the Channel several years ago.

Back to our original assumption that you own a fin-keel boat of moderately light displacement, with a sloop or cutter rig, low wetted surface, wide beam and not much under water. Under such circumstances, experience seems to indicate that running at high speed may well be the best answer in storm conditions. Eric Tabarly has used such tactics in the southern oceans and has survived. However, much would seem to depend on wave patterns and steepness. A boat with the above characteristics would be naturally buoyant, and would tend to ride the waves. But with the new designs that favor fine bows and a broad, flat stern, the chances of pitchpoling in particularly steep seas is something to think about before running hard.

It may well be wise to consider streaming warps aft. Lengths of your heaviest line (which for most sailors these days ain't much) should be belayed to the strongest fittings aft, and let overboard. Two 100-foot long, ¾-inch lines will have a remarkable effect, slowing a 30-footer by as much as two or three knots.

Heaving-to, the technique by which you back the jib or reefed main and lash the tiller to leeward, works only with a ship of reasonable lateral plane. It would be very difficult to get any modern fin-keeler to heave-to. More likely it would broach. A full-keeled or, I should say, long-keeled boat will do a much better job of it. The tiller (or wheel) must be lashed to a greater or lesser degree, which can be determined only by your experience with a particular boat. When all is set, the boat should forereach at a couple of knots. Traditionally, in the days when sail had the right of way, you could carry out this maneuver on the starboard tack (which is why, traditionally, the galley was to port). In our day, when no one pays the slightest attention to sailors except other sailors, heaving-to is not practiced much.

Certainly, in confined waters or on coastal passages it is not a tactic to be recommended unless some distance offshore, and not a lee shore at that. Rod Stephens told me he thought a number of the boats in the *Fastnet* disaster were caught out because they hadn't great enough lateral planes to attempt heaving-to. A CCA boat would have had a better chance.

Hulling, or lying ahull, is another heavy weather favorite, but there is certainly a lot of confusion about the subject. Richard Henderson, in *East to the Azores*, writes an informed and thoughtful section on this.

Figure 44. Heaving-to. Jib aback, reefed main just luffing, tiller lashed to leeward. When the boat is balanced, it should forereach at a knot or two. Good lateral plane is necessary for heaving-to to work.

Problems with hulling depend very much on the boat. A deep keel can cause tripping, sending you into a capsize (we are talking about extreme weather, remember). A shallow draft will probably be much more comfortable, though the leeway will be greater. In a centerboarder, the board should probably be raised, since the strains put upon hull and rigging are extreme. I find that my own boat, hulling in heavy weather, will not quite lie beam-on, but rather will point slightly upwind, causing some burying of the bows. However, as my boat is of fairly light displacement, I don't worry too much. It lifts to the seas.

The boat will take up whatever attitude it wishes on its own, and your attempts to alter that stance will probably spell disaster. A well-found and well-built modern boat will undoubtedly survive much greater abuse from the sea than one of Claude Worth's cutters, or even a boat like *Wanderer III*. Extreme heavy displacement will make for greater comfort, but I doubt that such a boat will be as safe in heavy going as a moderate or lightweight vessel. What is important in any vessel is reserve bouyancy fore and aft. Moderate overhangs with flare in the bows seems to be a wise idea. The stern shape doesn't matter a damn as long as the reserve is there and the run aft is clean.

I have run off in canoe sterns, transom sterns, all of them. The only trouble I had was in a Concordia yawl—which has a very fine stern indeed—and we got pooped twice. I have never been in a survival storm (and sincerely hope never to be), but have known sailors who have. In those conditions, simply staying afloat seems to be the major concern. No one has time to worry about the aesthetics or wave-breaking efficiency of the stern. It probably wouldn't matter anyhow.

Your first concern with seas and wind on the rise will be shortening sail. Once again, this is a matter of rig. In a cutter you can drop the jib, reef the main and keep going. In a sloop, reef the main and go to smaller and smaller jibs. Two-stick rigs will usually balance with foresail and mizzen, but I question the advisability of the combination. With such a rig the strains are great, and with a triatic stay, you are chancing loosing the mainmast. Better to reef the main and drop the mizzen, unless the mizzen is very small and can be used for balancing purposes.

Whatever, if you go more than a few miles offshore, the boat must have storm sails, and you must know how to use them.

A storm jib is no problem to rig, except that it must always be properly led aft. I prefer a permanently bent-on sheet with no hardware and screw-in deck blocks. The clew should be padded with leather or some other resilient material. The leads are important. A genoa track doesn't go far enough forward to be of any use, and it is too far outboard. Actually, a self-tending storm jib is possible with a rope traveler.

Remember to have your sailmaker install head and tack pennants of very stout wire.

A trysail is a most important bit of canvas, although very few are seen or used on this side of the Atlantic. However, when you need it, there is no substitute. It should be roped all around and should run up its own track for lacing around the mast, perhaps the best solution for the occasional singlehander. It should not sheet to the end of the boom. After all, you may wish to lash the boom to the house. Better to lead the sheets, also permanently bent on, to the quarters. Make sure your stern cleats are really substantial. You won't have to worry about winches because you will sheet a trysail flat. It becomes essentially self-tacking.

Both storm sails deserve the consideration of the best cloth and triple stitching. You may use them only once every ten years, but they could save your life and your ship. The fact that you will rarely use them makes it all the more important that you rehearse setting and dousing both. Back to the Fastnet. The report told of many crews who couldn't set storm sails. No provision had been made for them. You try hanking a storm jib on a grooved foil headstay! Sure the Fastnet storm was a freak; so was the hurricane of 1938, and thousands of squalls, despressions, cyclones and other oddments of Mother Nature.

Storm sails must be set before the storm, especially when singlehanding. Prudence and caution are the watchwords. Even 40 square feet of jib can batter you to utter exhaustion in 50-knot winds. Watch the weather, especially the barometer. When you have trouble sheeting in the working jib, change down. After two reefs, no main will be really effective, and the boom becomes a potential murderer. When the boat is over-canvassed with storm jib and double-reefed main, change down to trysail and jib, or trysail alone. If that's too much, survival tactics apply, and running under bare poles and/or with warps trailing may be the best lifesaver, if you have sea room.

10
Accidents and Emergencies

For a singlehander, nothing is more terrifying than going overboard. No man-overboard drills practiced with crew mean a damn thing. Prior preparation and practice is vital to saving one's life. Period. No exceptions.

Just before the beginning of the first OSTAR, Blondie Hasler was asked what would happen if someone fell overboard. Legend has it he replied, "I hope he would have the grace to drown like a gentleman." It is certainly one possibility, though not one I would like to consider.

Better to consider another activity plan, a what-would-I-do-if-it-actually-happened scenario. The obvious is to avoid going over the side at all costs. Wear a safety harness at night and whenever you leave the cockpit, even in moderate weather. Only one slip of the foot is necessary for disaster to strike. Safety harnesses are not comfortable. They are clumsy and awkward and dig in in all the wrong places. Some, however, work. In England, you can buy one with a *Kitemark*, which guarantees its having been tested according to British Government standards, which are very stringent.

Make sure that lifelines are high enough and that stanchions are really through-bolted. Most boats come with single lifelines. Get double ones. It is very easy to slip beneath one line. If the top lifeline is encased in vinyl, it will be easier to grab, but clear plastic allows you to inspect the wire. High enough? At least 24 inches, preferably 27 and ideally 30. I have seen a few ocean voyaging boats with 30-inch-high *triple* lines. That's careful planning.

Gates in lifelines are nice if you wear a kilt, but the weak link is the pelican hook closure. Gibb and Johnson both make safety catch hooks that I highly recommend and, should you decide on gates, be sure to install braces for the stanchions either side.

Wire lifelines running down the centerline have been discussed in the safety chapter, as have proper handrails.

Assuming you've done everything possible to stay in the boat, what happens if you still flip over the side? You've got to get back on board. Unless you're hand steering, the boat will continue on its merry way, not having any response to weather helm.

Precautions to take for getting back aboard include:

First, trail a polypropylene line—50 to 100 feet long—from a stern cleat. Tie a small buoy to the trailing end. Poly lines float, and if you can find one in a dayglow color, all the better.

Second, mount a ladder that is reachable from the stern. It can be a drop-down stainless steel one, or a rope with a release line. Assuming the boat is whizzing along at five or six knots, you will, with all your clothes, have a very difficult time hauling yourself to the stern. You will be exhausted. Even climbing a ladder will be a Herculean feat. If you happen to have a boat fitted with a transom-hung rudder, steps can be attached to the rudder blade. No matter what type of ladder you use, make sure the bottom two rungs sink well below the surface. Weight them if necessary with a small lead pig.

If you are equipped with self-steering, arrange a trailing line that will trip the steering gear. Another solution must be arrived at for vanes that do not employ tiller lines, especially those with separate, servo-assisted rudders.

Provided you are able to get back on board, you will be exhausted, cold, very wet and possibly on the verge of shock. If you're in clear waters, get below instantly, get out of *all* your clothes, put on the heaviest, warmest things you've got, especially for your feet and hands, and get something warm into your stomach. Don't drink alcohol! But soup, tea or cocoa will warm you with no after effects. Drink slowly and give your body time to build up its temperature again. Even ten minutes in temperate water (about 65° F) can lower your body temperature considerably, especially as you are losing even more body heat in your attempts to get back aboard.

Another area of concern to the singlehander is injuries or illness. I remember sailing dead downwind for eleven hours with a 102° F fever, trying to reach port, where I could get aid and assistance. I knew I had the flu, but I had no desire to fight it out alone in an isolated cove. During those eleven hours, I fell asleep three times. I was foolish and I did something that could have ended tragically. The boat was well stocked, I knew what was wrong with me and I should have stayed put for a couple of days. But I had to get back to the office.

The moral of the story is: be prepared. Have a good medical kit, learn how to administer basic first aid to yourself and think about how you will manage if you are *slightly* disabled. If you develop serious illness, or sustain serious bodily injury, obviously you must seek help by any means, and the quickest means possible. But if the damage is slight, you alone must decide if you are able to continue safely to your destination.

Your first aid kit is of vital importance. It is your only line of defense. Don't assume for a moment that the little plastic boxes with red crosses on top that you buy from your chandlery are adequate for more than cuts and scrapes. True, you will suffer from cuts and scrapes, occasional pulled muscles and sunburn most often. Nevertheless, it is essential that you buy a good marine first aid book. The two best are by Peter Eastman and Earl Rubell, both experienced sailor-physicians. Go over their suggested drug and medical supply lists with your own doctor, taking into account any particular physical and emotional problems you may suffer from. Then, armed with real information and a few prescriptions, visit your local druggist and place your purchases in a watertight plastic or metal container within easy reach of the companionway.

You will notice the mention of emotional problems. Sailors are supposed to be a hearty, rough bunch. However, they are also human. Fear, trepidation and insecurity are but a few of the problems common to many, and especially to singlehanders. Confidence doesn't come until you've done it. Your emotional state is 100 percent as important to successful passagemaking as is your physical well-being. Witness the tragic end to Donald Crowhearst, the round-the-world racer who tried to fool the world and ended up committing suicide.

The advice in the chapter on fatigue is good preventive medicine. Cuts and such deserve a Band-Aid. Headaches, two aspirin. But a broken arm, a head injury, a large gash or anything infected—not to mention symptoms of severe internal disorders—calls for immediate action. Don't say to yourself, "It'll go away." If you can't cope, GET OUTSIDE HELP IMMEDIATELY. Never let pride get in the way. Call up the Coast Guard, get the boat to the nearest port with a hospital as fast as possible or throw over the anchor and send out a distress message, either by radio or, lacking one, by flare or other visual distress signal.

You have no one to rely upon but yourself. Don't panic. Sit down and analyze the situation. Decide what you are really capable of. If the weather is deteriorating, make for the nearest port if you feel capable of the passage. Neither waste nor hoard time. Do for yourself what you would for a wife or child.

11
Anchoring and Docking Under Sail

Most sailors are used to anchoring under power with the reluctant help of their wives. A large number probably have never anchored at all, despite the hook and rode smartly displayed in the bows. This is a mistake, for not only does it keep you from the joys of peaceful anchorages, away from the peering eyes and stale air of marinas, but it is an important safety technique in a number of circumstances.

The first question the singlehander must ask is "Where to stow the hook?" The bow is, in a small boat, the worst place—it hampers performance and is *not* convenient. The coachroof isn't bad, but not particularly handy, either. I carry mine lashed either to the coachroof beside the companionway (in chocks) or lashed to the stern rail. The rode is run outside the lifelines, with about 75 feet clear to turn and the rest securely cleated. I come into an anchorage, drop the hook from the cockpit and let her fall back. If the hook doesn't dig in, I can always go forward. But, I always leave one sail up until the anchor's set, in any case.

As you might have guessed, I'm not overly fond of engines. Sure, they have their place: in calms, getting through narrow channels against the wind, maneuvering in very tight corners. Any sailor worth his salt should be able to pick up moorings and anchor or dock his vessel under sail. There may be times when you have to.

How you do any of the above under sail depends very much on your boat and its sailing characteristics. I find, especially in modern sloops and cutters, that coming in under just a small foresail, say a working jib, is best. First, you can let it fly, slowing the boat down appreciably. Second, it cannot be backed like a main, sending you scurrying off in the opposite direction. Third, you can't get smacked in the head, as with the main boom. Needless to say, at no time during any of these maneuvers should any sheets be cleated. A couple of turns on a winch and a single wrap around a cleat allows you to haul or ease at will, and both boat speed and direction will be affected by the trim of the jib.

This isn't to say you shouldn't use the engine, just that at least one driving sail must be kept set for safety's sake. Not a mizzen, and whatever it is that is hoisted—main or foresail—it should be large enough to allow maneuverability in the prevailing conditions, not too small and not too large. If no time exists for the fine points, stick to something too large. It's easier to spill wind than create it.

A roller furling or, better yet, a reefing headsail can be a godsend in singlehanded maneuvering. Since there is no such thing as ultimate reliability, a roller arrangement may well be the answer for you. Certainly, it is to be seriously considered if you are past the point where you enjoy dashing to the foredeck, lunging after runaway canvas. Be sure to keep the deck drum well lubricated. Mounted at the stemhead, it is more subject to corrosion and malfunction than anything else on the boat. And despite what manufacturers may say about "maintenance-free performance," fresh water rinsing and a good dollop of one of the modern Teflon or silicone lubricants can be worth its weight in gold. Bearings must not be allowed to get salty, otherwise you'll end up with an unbalanced drum with frozen bearings, and a broken gear.

In any case, whatever you choose, keep to only one sail. Handling more in any kind of weather can be truly frightening, especially when the wind is against the tide. Under those conditions, the main can back, the stern can swing around and general mayhem can ensue. Also, you avoid a tangle of sheets in the cockpit, and handling the tiller or wheel and two sets of sheets can cause anxiety out of all proportion to the task at hand.

As I mentioned previously, a staysail is both the pain and joy aboard a cutter. If it's boomed, it becomes the perfect anchoring sail, provided the total area can drive the boat in the prevailing conditions. Too often, staysails are of an undernourished size. This, combined with the rather aft position of the sail, can create an unnerving lee helm, especially on a heavy boat.But most modern vessels are of light to moderate displacement, which is probably better for sailing around the coasts of the United States. A moderate boat with lots of sail is far more maneuverable than the clunky Colin Archers or Pilot Cutter renditions being passed off as cruising boats.

Whatever sail you finally set, the old saw about reaching into the anchorage usually applies. You come in on a reach, knowing your boat's handling characteristics, and turn up to the spot where you'll drop your hook or pick up the mooring—remembering that wind and sea conditions, as well as boat speed and displacement, will affect coasting distances and times. Don't be dismayed if you don't get it right initially. But allow room to try again.

There are times when you must approach an anchorage from downwind or to windward. If you beat up to the hole, you simply luff and drop. Downwind is another matter. If your boat can spin on a dime, you may have enough boat speed to allow a head-to-wind approach at the last moment. If not, drop the hook from the stern. However, do this only with jib up. If you try this maneuver with the main winging out, the chances are the boat will drag the hook or you will beach the boat.

Do not drop the hook from the stern when anchoring downwind unless the rode is cleated first to the bow and then the stern. When the boat swings head-to-wind it can foul the rode if payed out from the bow. Once it holds and sails are doused, you can uncleat the stern and the boat should swing about right smartly.

Remember:

1. Ready anchor and rode on foredeck; make sure anchor is securely lashed but ready for quick release.
2. Assess anchorage for protection, windage, holding ground.
3. Double-check chart for optimum location, safety and permissibility.
4. Sail into anchorage, preferably under jib alone.
5. In your approach, try for a reach or, second best, a beat.
6. Sail to roughly the point you wish to drop the hook.
7. Turn the bows into the wind.
8. Move forward with care.
9. Unlash the anchor and let it over the side after the boat has lost forward momentum.
10. Pay out enough line for the type of holding ground and depth.
11. Snub the anchor and doubly secure the bitter end.

12. Take bearings of your position using three structures on shore for future reference.
13. Lower and stow all sail.
14. Secure wheel or tiller.
15. Clean up boat and have a drink.

The technique for sailing into a dock or picking up a mooring isn't much different, except that you must be somewhat more aware of the boat's velocity and your ability to make it stop when you want it to. This is largely a factor of wind speed versus sail area versus sheer displacement. A heavy boat is a lot slower to respond to slacked sheets than a light flyer. You will learn this with practice, and it's well worth the effort. You can never predict when your ever-dependable diesel will conk out—usually, of course, just when you need it. Engines are particularly subject to Murphy's Law.

No matter what, never let the wind get behind you approaching any solid structure—pontoon, dock, wall and so on. Invariably the structure has the advantage over the boat. Net result: one crumpled bow!

12
Ship Management

Under this heading comes everything involved with keeping the ship and you shipshape. Included are a number of items usually left to the crew and mate. You have two choices: learn or don't learn. Eat cans of stew and find cookie crumbs at the bottom of your sleeping bag, your ropes in Gordian knots and your socks with gaping holes. Or, you can see to it that both captain and vessel are kept Bristol fashion.

The practical advantages of keeping things in order are simple: you can find what you want when you need it, plan your store replenishment accordingly and save time and money. Psychologically, you will find yourself better organized, less subject to fatigue and in better spirits.

If an army crawls on its stomach, a sailor can be said to haul ropes on his. Since you are going to be alone, you might as well learn something about eating and stewardship. A case of hash, a loaf of bread and a jar of instant coffee do not make for good nutrition or good eating. I covered some of the precepts of nutrition on the water in the chapter on fatigue. Following are some ideas that may make things easier and certainly tastier for the novice sea cook.

Eating well is the best revenge

This is no place for a collection of dubious recipes. Loads of cruising cookbooks exist, though the reason escapes me. They all seem to reflect the notion that two cans and a dash of ketchup equals "gourmet" paradise. Bull!

First, learn to use your stove. Second, equip it with really sturdy pot clamps. Third, get one extra-heavy pot with a tightly fitting lid and parallel sides, and six inches or so in depth. You're set. Obviously, what you eat depends on your culinary skills, habits and appetite. But there is no reason to subsist on Spam and saltines.

Just like everything else, the key to good food aboard is planning. If you intend to cruise for a week, stock up for that time with *fresh* foods. Eggs, vegetables, fruit, meat, all will keep for at least that long. Only the meat needs refrigeration. And with country-cured hams and bacon you can get by with hanging them from a carlin, covered in cheesecloth. Cheese is a great standby, as are dried fruits and nuts. I have a passion for chocolate bars, pumpernickel bread and stuffed grape leaves. None of these needs refrigeration and each supplies something valuable in the way of nutrients.

Stow everything with care, even in the icebox. Tossing about will ruin the best produce in no time at all. The deep sink I've mentioned will hold anything better than the highest fiddles, especially mugs for hot liquids.

Whatever you plan, try to eat when you are hungry. Three meals per day are great if you live that way at home. Personally, I find my energy level remains much higher if I eat when my stomach not my habits tells me to. Keep a thermos of hot water (filled after morning coffee) to supply you throughout the sail with instant soups, Cup O'Noodles, cocoa or hot toddies.

A Mini-Galley or Sea-Swing stove are perfect for quick snacks. Also, don't leave dirty dishes lying around. Keep things clean and neat. In heavy weather you'll come to appreciate your housekeeping foresight. In the same vein, try not to stow cardboard boxes anywhere without wrapping them first in plastic bags. I remember one morning, on a friend's boat, opening a locker to find a mass of cornflakes treading water. Not the way I wanted to start the day.

Unless you have open water and gentle breezes ahead—very rarely do such conditions exist—plan on one-pot meals. You would be surprised at the enormous variety you can concoct. A few examples:

Stew—oil, onions, potatoes, meat or poultry, broth or juice or wine, spices. Brown chopped onions in oil, then add chunks of meat and brown. Next add liquid and cut-up potatoes and spice as you like (salt, pepper, herbs, curry, vinegar, etc, but not all at once, please). Cover and simmer until all are tender.

Hot cereals—in bad weather a godsend. Prepare oatmeal, cornmeal, whatever, as per package. Add chunks of ham, sausage (pre-cooked) or corned beef, with lots of fresh pepper and butter.

Pasta—add about a third of a pound of pasta to salted, rapidly boiling water. Cook al dente (still firm). Drain and add oil or melt butter in the same pot. Add shrimp, cooked chicken or meat, plenty of grated Parmesan and a bit of garlic. Eat with a salad and some wine.

Toasted sandwiches—ham, cheese, tomato, onion, between two slices of any kind of bread. Sauté, pressing down with a spatula until the bread is browned and the cheese melts.

Simple choucroute garni—heat sauerkraut with sausages, ham, white wine and peppercorns. Eat with white wine and plenty of bread.

As seen from the above, ingredients can be simple and preparation will take less than half an hour, although cooking time will vary with the stove, pot thickness, and so on. With a touch of imagination, literally hundreds of nourishing, good tasting meals can be prepared with little fuss. Ernest K. Gann, the author and sailor, lives on Dinty Moore Stew. Let that be his problem. Eat well instead.

Keeping the boat working

Once you're well fed, you will have the energy to keep everything else functioning. Four areas demand general and constant attention: head, cabin, engine room and deck. We might as well start with the sacred head.

In the United States, you must by law conform to the government regulations concerning overboard discharge of human waste. Basically, you may use a holding tank system, have a macerator/chlorinator type head or use a portable head. This applies to all permanently installed toilets in any boat within three miles of the continental land mass of this country. In the Great Lakes and other inland bodies of water, regulations permit no dumping whatsoever.

With the exception of portable heads, these systems are expensive, consume power and, in the case of holding tanks, use up one hell of a lot of space. You know my other solution: the bucket. It is not permanently mounted. Therefore, it can be used with abandon. One-third filled with sea water, and dumped overboard after each use, the bucket remains sweet and can be stowed anywhere.

Cedar used to be the preferred material, but such devices now cost about $40. Plastic is not to be encouraged. It holds odors and, when scratched, is very hard to keep sanitary. I use a stainless steel vessel of awesome beauty with a seat I cut out of plywood and varnished.

Whichever method is used, keep a supply of biodegradable toilet paper on hand. Nothing is more unpleasant than taking a head apart to unclog it. Household tissue will do it in no time. Also keep a set of spares for gaskets, diaphragms and such stowed by the head. A splendid way to maintain sweetness and smooth operation is to squirt ordinary dishwashing detergent into the bowl once a week and pump vigorously.

Cabins are used to live in, sleep in and eat in. A place for everything and everything in its place is an old saw, but true enough, especially within the small confines of a cruising boat. Air the bedding daily and stow it. Clean the saloon table before casting off. Don't leave books, old socks and lanterns lying around settees. They will end up on the floor, soaked. Place navigational instruments in racks. A flying compass can relieve you of an ear.

In other words, behave like a sailor, not a slob. Just because you are alone is no reason to neglect what is, in actuality, good seamanship.

Engine rooms, or engine resting places, are the most neglected area of any auxiliary. They collect grease, oil, odd bolts, rusted tools and frayed wire ends. Again the rule is: Keep it clean and organized. Engine pans should be mopped regularly, stray dirt and grime wiped off the block, spares carried—plugs and ignition parts for gasoline engines, impellers for diesels. Better yet, have the engine maker make up a spare parts kit. You need tools at the ready which fit the various bolt heads and pipes sticking out all over. An engine with hand-starting capability is a great boon, especially as batteries have a way of dying when you must need them. These, by the way, should be tightly strapped into boxes, well ventilated and away from seawater (the combination can produce hydrogen gas).

Finally, the most important and most neglected area of shipkeeping—the deck. Here is where you spend most of your time, where most hazards exist, what your neighbors most see. Keep it neat. Coil lines, tie off halyards, brake the wheel or tie the tiller, use chafe gear, wipe up the peanut butter and make sure all deck fittings are tightly fastened and functioning. Cover the mainsail. Tighten the mainsheet and don't leave anything loose to blow away or be kicked overboard.

If you think about it, all the areas of ship management concern your eventual safety. The boat can go down to the gurgle of an open seacock; an engine won't start as you are heading toward a tanker; or something sharp flying off a table, incapacitating you, are all potential disasters. Care and concern in keeping things as they should be will pay off.

Appendices

A
Dinghies

Hard or inflatable, towed or hoisted aboard, a dinghy is your lifeline to shore. And, if you don't have a life raft aboard, it is your major buoyancy aid as well.

If your boat is under 35 feet, you will not be able to carry a solid dink unless the foredeck is flush or the space between companionway and mast is long and clear (no lines back to the cockpit here!). Your options include davits or towing. Davits are dangerous for two reasons—they are vulnerable to following seas and they add considerable weight aft. In the days of heavy displacement, this was fine, but a few hundred pounds hanging from the afterdeck of a 10,000-pound boat will have an appreciable effect on performance. Also, both davits and deck stowage add an enormous amount of windage, and will probably hamper your progress to windward.

Towing is fine, killing only a knot or less from boat speed. However, the strains on deck gear, towline and bow fittings of the dink are enormous. Also, someone has to keep an eye on the dink. Weaving back and forth, surging, flipped or driven into the stern of the mother ship, a towed dink is a poor traveling companion in my opinion. Others will disagree, but when alone, you have enough to worry about without adding the bother of a trailing albatross.

Having gone through all the possibilities, I have come to settle on a good inflatable—Zodiac, Avon, Achilles, Beaufort, Dunlop, etc.—for ease of stowage, stability (important, when alone, to a greater degree than you might imagine) and convenience. Sure, they don't row like a peapod or a good skiff, but they don't create any problems when you are *not* using them. They demand absolutely no attention when you're under sail.

I don't like small motors. They are inconvenient to stow and mount, leak gas and generally get in the way. If you feel too decrepit to handle oars, then get one by all means. If you wish to use oars, buy ones with leathers and solid oarlocks, made preferably of spruce. Ash oars are the norm and they are twice the weight of spruce. That makes quite a difference on a long haul to shore.

Inflatables give you less choice, and the strokes used must be modified—short and strong rather than the long and easy strokes used rowing a boat. Make sure you always carry a bailer and a small anchor (well protected in blow-up boats—the folding Norwegian type is good) with rode. You may come across an unknown current and not be able to fight it, even with a motor. Floorboards are necessary for inflatables, and handholds for row boats. Thwarts must be adjustable and foot braces are lovely if you can fit them.

Your inflatable should be clearly identified and easy to handle alone. A 300-pound rowing skiff has no place in a singlehander's inventory.

B
Damage and Repair

The damage you are most likely to suffer is grounding and, perhaps, holing. If no opening has appeared when you go aground and you're not taking in any water, your first task is to refloat the ship. Kedging is probably your best bet after attempting backing sails and motoring in reverse. Get an anchor out to deeper water and start winching. Your weight alone will not be able to shift the boat and you should stay in the cockpit to control things once the boat floats free. Either swim the anchor out on a life jacket or horseshoe or row it out. If the tide is rising, have a drink.

If damage has been sustained, you are going to have to stop the leak somehow. Minor ones can be pumped and pumped until you can get help. If the water has come to the floorboards, bail with a bucket and try to locate the entry. Usually ruptures and breaks can be best sealed from outside. If you go over, hook on a safety line and take something to stuff into the break. On a wooden boat, a patch can be nailed over the outside of the opening. On a glass boat, you'll have more problems. Nothing works well, though I've heard of very good results with umbrella patches and good old plumbers helpers. Suction may be your best bet. Imaginative improvisation is an absolute must.

Rigging damage is the other great fear, which is one reason some offshore sailors like ketch rigs—one mast will probably remain standing. However, a single stick of adequate section and rigging, well cared for, will take an awful lot of abuse. If a stay or shroud goes, switch tacks or run or beat to take the strain off that particular wire until you can get sails down and rig a spare or, lacking that, a rope substitute. Then proceed under appropriate and reduced canvas. If the mast goes, cut it free (cable cutters and hacksaw needed). It is unlikely that, alone, you will be able to save it. Just too much weight. The boom can be salvaged to make a jury rig though. Of course, all this assumes you are offshore. Inshore you can simply motor to your nearest boatyard. Carefully plan any move involving mast or rigging. You are in mortal danger when grappling with the forces generated by gyrating masts and wind-whipped wires. Think out every move first and make sure you are secured to the boat with a safety harness. At night, set up a deck light of sufficient brilliance to illuminate the entire deck, if possible. If nothing works, then call for help.

C
Wind-powered Self-steering Devices

Following is a list of vanes generally available, with notes on type and application, and, in some cases, addresses of manufacturers.

Aries: Horizontally pivoted vane operating servo-pendulum with lines to tiller, suitable for boats to 50 feet. One of the most tried and tested of all, used aboard the Hiscocks' *Wanderer IV*. Simple and very strong. Marine Vane Gears Ltd., Northwood, Cowes, IOW, UK.

Atmos: Horizontally pivoted vane operating servo-pendulum, for boats to 40 feet. Lightweight, proven vane of French manufacture.

Crew: This unusual Norwegian gear uses a Bowden cable linkage, so it can be easily mounted anywhere. Obviously there will be some friction problems and careful maintenance is necessary. Norway.

Gunning: Several different models of direct and servo-pendulum gears for boats ranging from pocket cruisers to 65 footers. Robust and well-proven. Morriss Marine, Saltmarsh Lane, Hayling Island, Hants., UK.

Hasler: The granddaddy of them all. Vertical pivot vane, servo-pendulum to tiller/wheel, suitable for boats to 50 feet. Several models for different size boats, different rudder arrangements. M.S. Gibb Ltd., Warsash, Southampton, UK.

Hydrovane: Vane horizontally pivoted to auxiliary rudder, suitable for yachts up to 50 feet. In production for 15 years. Hydrovane Yacht Equipment Ltd, Woolverstone Marina, Woolverstone, Suffolk, UK.

MNOP: This highly sophisticated vane is horizontally pivoted to a trim tab and permanently mounted auxiliary rudder. Developed by Marcel Gianoli (Eric Tabarly's vane man), it is very expensive and very sensitive. France.

Mustafa: Similar to the MNOP gear, the Mustafa can be fitted to boats up to 60 feet. It is very powerful, very sensitive, very quick-acting, very expensive. The auxiliary rudder comes fitted with an emergency tiller that can be used for steering should the main rudder become disabled. Italy.

Navik: Horizontally pivoted vane with servo-pendulum, for yachts to 45 feet. Lightweight and frail looking, but eminently successful in OSTAR racing. Several accessories available: remote vane adjustment, long shaft servo blade. Plastimo, France.

Number One: Similar to QME, but leads are designed to negate crossover with tacking. Number One Marine, 56 Sutton Mill Road, Potton, Bedfordshire, UK.

QME: Direct vane-to-tiller/wheel, horizontally pivoted. Suitable for well-balanced boats to 30 feet. Quantock Marine Enterprises, Church Street, Bridgewater, Somerset, UK.

Ratcliffe: One of the few makers who insist on custom fitting and design for each individual boat. All types of gears short of the Mustafa type are available. Quality work and after-installation service. Highly recommended. 173 Washington Street, Pembroke, MA 02359.

RVG: Vane vertically pivoted to trimtab to auxiliary rudder. Simpler than the MNOP and the Mustafa above, the RVG is robust and reliable, though not quite as sensitive. Several sizes for yachts up to 60 feet. Riebandt Vane Steering, P.O. Box 2153, Idyllwild, CA 92349.

Sailomat: Horizontally pivoted vane operating a servo-pendulum and auxiliary rudder, suitable for yachts to 55 feet. One of the most sophisticated vanes, with a price to match; highly sensitive, even downwind. Sailomat, Sweden.

Saye's Rig: Vertical axis vane operating a servo tab. This gear employs an unusual, direct tab-to-rudder connection that allows easy shipping of the tab assembly. Reliable. Roland Saye, P.O. Box 1994, Newport Beach, CA 92663.

Vectis Vane Gear: Horizontally pivoted vane operating servo-pendulum, tiller lines. Well-engineered and -built, though not cheap.

Vectis Vane Gears, Little London, Newport, IOW, UK.
Windpilot: Vertically pivoted vane operating auxiliary rudder, suitable for boats up to 35 feet. One of the simplest of the auxiliary rudder vanes, well tested. German.

D
Spares and Tools

Following, courtesy of Jeff Neuberth, is a list, or rather three lists, of spare parts, tools and oddments that might well be carried aboard any boat, but especially offshore, when you have no one but yourself to undertake repairs.

Boats Under 30 Feet

TOOLS
8″ adjustable wrench
medium sized pliers
medium blade screwdriver
10″ vise grips
pocket rigging knife with spike
Dacron pouch or waterproof bag to carry tools

SAIL REPAIR KIT
scissors
sailmaker's wax
palm
seam ripper
hot knife
three spools waxed polyester
needles (5 each #'s 15 & 17)
one roll Rip-stop tape
3′ × 3′ piece of adhesive sticky-back Dacron
light thread for spinnaker repair, telltale yarn
nylon dittybag containing all of the above

SPARE PARTS
assorted stainless steel nuts, bolts, washers, sheet metal screws
bulbs for compass and running lights
winch pawls and springs
cam cleat springs
cotter pins (stainless steel, two of each size used and split rings)
small clear plastic tackle box to contain above

ODDS AND ENDS
one roll of silver duct tape (Nashua 357)
tube of clear silicone seal
one can WD-40
small can 3-in-1 oil
Magic Marker (black)
can of (Moly Coat) Never-Seize
nylon dittybag to hold the above

For Boats From 30′ To 45′

TOOLS
Allen wrenches
chisels (one cold)
drills (hand drill plus set of bits)
files (8″ mill bastard, one medium size rattail, one triangular)
hammer (medium ballpeen)
50′ measuring tape
nail set
oil stone
pliers (channel locks, needle nose, 2 regular)
saw (hacksaw plus at least 10 high-speed blades)
screwdrivers (6 assorted sized regular, 2 Phillips head, 1 jeweler's set)
vise grips (7″ and 10″)
wire brush
wire cutters (medium sized Felco's)
work gloves
wrenches (8″ and 10″ adjustable, set of combination—open end and box)
wooden tool box or dry organized area to store all of the above

ELECTRICAL PARTS
spare bulb for each light aboard
three each spare fuses for each kind aboard
assorted wire crimps
wire stripper/crimpers
flashlight batteries and bulbs
continuity tester
black electrical tape

ENGINE AND MECHANICAL SPARES
three cans of oil for hydraulics
hydraulic hose and assorted end fittings
transmission fluid
set of engine filters
assorted grits wet/dry sandpaper
complete set engine belts
enough oil for oil change
new voltage regulator for each alternator
6′×6′ canvas drop cloth with grommets
piece of plywood
piece of wood (2×4)
assorted hose clamps
drift punch

SPARES
assorted nuts, bolts and washers
five of each size cotter key used aboard
assorted clevis pins
assorted "D" shackles
assorted snap shackles
one standing rigging toggle
one genoa car
winch pawls
winch pawl springs
winch roller bearings

SAIL REPAIR KIT
scissors
sailmaker's wax
two palms
two seam rippers
hot knife
light thread for spinnaker repairs
six spools waxed polyester
needles (10 each #'s 13,15, 17,19)
Rip-stop tape

3′×6′ piece of sticky-back Dacron
yarn for telltales
25′ seizing wire
three "D" rings
sailmaker's pliers
nylon bag to hold all of the above

SEALERS AND LUBRICANTS
two-part epoxy
two tubes clear silicone seal
two cans WD-40
can CRC 666
can 3-in-1 oil
silicone spray
special grease mixture
rolls of colored tape
two rolls of duct tape
Magic Markers (black)
one can Felpro C5A

Tools For Yachts 45′ and Larger

Allen wrenches (long and short)
awls (small and large)
block plane
chisels (one cold, two regular)
drills (brace, hand drill, 3/8″ chuck variable-speed reversible electric drill, two sets of metal bits)
files (8″, 10″, 12″ mill bastards, three wood files, two rattails, one triangular)
hammers (16 oz. ballpeen, baby sledge, claw and rubber mallet)
measuring (100′ measuring tape, fold-up ruler, calipers)
mirror (one retrieving)
nail sets (five assorted)
oil stone
pipe cutter
pipe length (for battering ram)
pliers (two channel locks, two needle nose, four regular in assorted sizes)
putty knives (two 1″)
saws (cross cut, hacksaw and 40 blades, jigsaw and 12 blades)
screwdrivers (17 assorted regular, six assorted Phillips head, two off-set, one set of jewelers)
tap and die set (including 8-32, 10-24, 10-32, 1/4-20, 5/16-24, 3/8-16, 3/8-24)
tin snips
torch set (complete Bernzomatic)
vise
vise grips (7″ and 10″)
wire brushes
wire cutters (large and small Felco's, large and small Dikes)
work gloves
wrenches (6″, 8″, 10″ adjustables; 14″ pipe wrench, strap wrench, complete 3/8″ drive socket set, complete set combination wrenches, popular-sized open-end wrenches)
X-Acto knife and six blades
wooden tool box to contain the above

ELECTRICAL PARTS
compass light assembly
running light bulbs
spare bulb for each brand of light aboard
three of each kind of fuse aboard
assorted wire crimps

wire stripper-crimpers
flashlight batteries and bulbs
assorted sizes of wire
black electrical tape
silicone grease
multimeter
solder
soldering gun or iron
spare anemometer cups
spare wind vane
spare knotmeter transducers
tackle box for the above

SEALERS AND LUBRICANTS

two part epoxy
two tubes clear silicone sealer
two cans WD-40
two cans CRC 666
two non-aerosol cans 3-in-1 oil
two cans silicone spray
special grease mixture
one can Felpro C5A
two rolls duct tape
two rolls of each colored tape
two Magic Markers (black)
Dacron bag to hold the above

SAIL REPAIR KIT

scissors
sailmaker's wax
two palms
two seam rippers
hot knife and spare tip
light thread for spinnaker repairs
eight spools waxed polyester
needles (one package each of #'s 13,15,17,19)
two rolls Rip-stop spinnaker repair tape
two 3′×6′ pieces sticky-backed Dacron
yarn (red, green and blue for telltales)
two weights seizing wire (25′ each)
three "D" or "O" rings
50′ tubular webbing
sailmaker's pliers
assorted weight sailcloth
roll 5 oz. Dacron tape, 6″ width
spool 5⁄32″ flag halyard
six awls
grommet set (stud, spur, mallet, die, rings, liners)
Dacron bag to hold the above

RIGGING PARTS

Nico-press tool (size of halyards, two preferable)
12 Nico-press sleeves for each size wire aboard
assorted stainless steel thimbles
assorted snap shackles
assorted "D" shackles
several lengths different weight wire (15″ each)
assorted rigging toggles
assorted clevis pins
assorted track cars
link plate set
spare main halyard
spare genoa halyard
good size turnbuckle
plastic fishing tackle box for above

ENGINE & MECHANICAL SPARES

gallon of oil for hydraulic rigging adjusters
10′ length hydraulic hose, assorted fittings
two cans transmission fluid
oil for engine oil change
set engine filters, gaskets
complete set engine belts
voltage regulator for each alternator

6′ × 6′ canvas drop cloth with grommets
assorted hose clamps
piece of plywood
two pieces 3′ long 2 × 4s
drift punch
set of injectors
grease gun with special grease
two cans starting spray (Ether)
keel bolt wrench
rudder-packing wrench
spare set steering cables
master links (12) for steering chain and spinnaker pole chain

WINCH PARTS
12 pawls
24 pawl springs
assorted roller bearings
six split rings
tooth brush
tweezers
dental pick
extra handle
clear plastic box to hold the above

SPARES
clear plastic tackle box containing 12 of each size SS cotter pins
clear plastic box of nuts, bolts, and washers (12 each size including #'s 6, 8, 12 and ¼″, 5⁄16″, ⅜″)
head repair kit: spare pump parts, diaphragms, impellers
hand pump for bilge, for changing oil
electric drill pump, hoses
sleeve bronze wool
12 sheets each wet/dry sandpaper in 220, 400, 600 grits
three sheets each crocus cloth, emery paper
spare packing for propeller and rudder glands

OPTIONAL
banding tool, bands, and clips

E
Suggested First Aid Kit by Earl Rubell, M.D.

Injectables

Decadron solution, 4 mg per ml*
Adrenalin (epinephrine 1 to 1000)*
Demerol, 4 mg per ml*
Sterile 2-ml syringes with 23-gauge needles*
Sterile 1-ml syringes with 25-gauge needles*

Injuries

Assorted sizes of Band-Aids
Sterile packages of 2 × 2-inch and 4 × 4-inch sterile gauze pads
Adhesive tape
Sterile roller gauze of the self-clinging type
Cotton balls
Q-tips
Box of assorted finger splints
Wrist splints, right-handed and left-handed
Betadine solution
Package of Steri-Strips
Package of sterile Vaseline gauze
Suture set, packaged and sterile. Needle holder, thumb forceps, scissors
Sterile packages of #4-0 silk suture material on swedged-on needles
1% Xylocaine local anesthetic solution*

*Requires a prescription

Seasickness

Dramamine
Marezine
Triptone
Bucladin*

Pain (oral medications)

Aspirin, 5-grain tablets or capsules
Acetaminophen (Tylenol, Datril, Phenaphen, Tempra), 5-grain tablets or capsules
Empirin Compound with Codeine #3*
Acetaminophen with Codeine #3*
Pyridium, 100-mg tablets*

Infection

Erythromycin, 400-mg* or capsules
Gantrisin, 500-mg tablets*
Ampicillin, 500-mg tablets*
Tetracycline, 250-mg* or capsules
Nafcillin, 500-mg tablets*
Chloroquine tablets (for malaria only)*

Allergies

Chlor-Trimeton, 4-mg tablets

Digestive Disorders

Lomotil tablets (syrup for children)*
Colace tablets (syrup for children)
Fleet enema (pediatric strength for children)
Glycerin suppositories

*Requires a prescription

Enema bag or rectal bulb syringe
Pepto-Bismol
Tigan, 200-mg suppositories*

Respiratory Disorders

Cough medicine. Any mild nonprescription medication
Phenergan Expectorant with Codeine*
Nose drops or nasal spray. Any brand
Antihistamine/decongestant ("cold remedy")—any brand that does not contain aspirin

Poisoning

Syrup of Ipecac

Sedation

Valium, 5-mg tablets*

Local Applications (eyes, ears, skin)

Visine eye drops
10% Sulamyd ophthalmic solution*
Cortisporin otic solution*
Sun filter cream with para-aminobenzoic acid (PABA)
Vaseline
Desenex ointment and powder
Neosporin ointment
Rubbing alcohol
Hydrocortisone cream or lotion
Lotrimin cream*

*Requires a prescription

Miscellaneous Equipment

Oxygen tank and mask
Snake bite kit

Index

Page numbers for figures are in parentheses